OSTEND

OSTEND

Stefan Zweig, Joseph Roth,
and the Summer Before the Dark

• • •

VOLKER WEIDERMANN

Translated from the German
by Carol Brown Janeway

PANTHEON BOOKS, NEW YORK

All rights reserved. Published in the United States by Pantheon Books,
a division of Penguin Random House LLC, New York, and distributed in
Canada by Random House of Canada, a division of Penguin Random House
Canada Ltd., Toronto. Originally published in Germany as *Ostende: 1936,
Sommer der Freundschaft* by Verlag Kiepenheuer & Witsch, Cologne, in 2014.
Copyright © 2014 by Verlag Kiepenheuer & Witsch.

Pantheon Books and colophon are registered trademarks
of Penguin Random House LLC.

*Grateful acknowledgment is made to the following for permission to reprint previ-
ously published material:* A. S. Kline: Excerpt from "The Violet" by Johann
Wolfgang von Goethe, translated by A. S. Kline, translation copyright © 2004
by A. S. Kline. All rights reserved. Reprinted by permission of A. S. Kline.
Stephen Mitchell: Excerpt from *The Lay of the Love and Death of Cornet
Christoph Rilke*, by Rainer Maria Rilke, translated by Stephen Mitchell.
Reprinted by permission of Stephen Mitchell.

Library of Congress Cataloging-in-Publication Data
Weidermann, Volker, [date]
[Ostend. English]
Ostend : Stefan Zweig, Joseph Roth, and the summer before the dark /
Volker Weidermann ; translated from the German by Carol Brown Janeway.
pages ; cm
ISBN 978-1-101-87026-6 (hardcover). ISBN 978-1-101-87027-3 (eBook).
1. Authors, German—Homes and haunts—Belgium—Ostend. 2. Authors,
Austrian—Homes and haunts—Belgium—Ostend. 3. Authors, exiled—
Belgium—Ostend. 4. Zweig, Stefan, 1881–1942—Friends and associates.
5. Roth, Joseph, 1894–1939—Friends and associates. 6. Keun, Irmgard,
1905–1982—Friends and associates. 7. Ostend (Belgium)—Social life
and customs. 8. Nineteen thirty-six, A.D. I. Janeway, Carol Brown,
translator. II. Title.
PT405.W3513613 2015 838'.91209—dc23 2015019901

www.pantheonbooks.com

Jacket images: (top, right) Stefan Zweig: Imagno/Hulton Archive/
Getty Images; (middle, left) Joseph Roth: Granger, N.Y.C.; (bottom)
Port of Ostend: Library of Congress, Washington, D.C.
Jacket design by Oliver Munday

Printed in the United States of America
First American Edition
2 4 6 8 9 7 5 3 1

OSTEND

· · ·

IT'S SUMMER UP HERE by the sea; the gaily colored bathing huts glow in the sun. Stefan Zweig is sitting in a loggia on the fourth floor of a white house that faces onto the broad boulevard of Ostend, looking at the water. It's one of his recurrent dreams, being here, writing, gazing out into the emptiness, into summer itself. Right above him, on the next floor up, is his secretary, Lotte Altmann, who is also his lover; she'll be coming down in a moment, bringing the typewriter, and he'll dictate his *Buried Candelabrum* to her, returning repeatedly to the same sticking point, the place from which he cannot find a way forward. That's how it's been for some weeks now.

Perhaps his great friend Joseph Roth will have some advice. His friend, whom he's going to meet later in the bistro, as he does every afternoon this summer. Or one of the others, one of the detractors, one of the fighters, one of the cynics, one of the drinkers, one of the blow-hards, one of the silent onlookers. One of the group that sits downstairs on the boulevard of Ostend, waiting for the moment when they can go back to their homeland. Racking their brains over what they can do to change the world's trajectory so that they can go home to the country they came from, so that in turn they can maybe even come back here to this beach on a visit one day, as guests. For now, they're refugees in vacationland. The apparently ever-cheerful Hermann Kesten, the preacher Egon Erwin Kisch, the bear Willi Muenzenberg, the champagne queen Irmgard Keun, the great swimmer Ernst Toller, the strategist Arthur Koestler: friends, foes, storytellers thrown together here overlooking the beach in July by the vagaries of world politics. And the stories they tell will be the fragments shored against their ruin.

Stefan Zweig in the summer of 1936. He looks at the sea through the large window and thinks with a mixture of pity, reticence, and pleasure about the group of displaced men and women he will be rejoining shortly. Until a few years ago, his life had been pure ascent—simple, greatly admired, and greatly envied. Now he's afraid, he feels himself bound by a hundred obligations, a hundred invisible fetters. Nothing will loosen them, nothing will provide support. But there is this summer, in which everything might change. Here, on this extravagantly wide boulevard with its magnificent white house and its great casino, the extraordinary Palace of Luck. Holiday mood, lively atmosphere, ice creams, parasols, lethargy, wind, wooden booths.

He was here once before; it was the summer of 1914, when the disaster began; with the headlines and the newsboys all along the beach promenade screaming more excitedly with every day that passed, excited and joyous because they were doing the best business they'd ever had.

The majority of the bathers who tore the papers out of their hands were German. The boys yelled the headlines: RUSSIA PROVOKES AUSTRIA; GERMANY PREPARES TO MOBILIZE. And Zweig too—pale, well dressed, with wire-rimmed glasses—came down by tram to be closer to the unfolding news. He was electrified by the headlines; they made him feel delightfully aroused and excited. Of course he knew that the whole drama would subside into a general silence soon enough, but right now he simply wanted to savor it. The possibility of a great event. The possibility of a war. The possibility of a grand future, of an entire world in motion. His joy was especially great when he looked into the faces of his Belgian friends. They had turned pale in the course of these last days. They were unprepared to join the game and seemed to be taking the whole thing very seriously. Stefan Zweig laughed. He laughed over the pathetic troops of Belgian soldiers on the promenade. Laughed over a little dog that was dragging a machine gun along behind it. Laughed over the entire holy solemnity of his friends.

He knew they had nothing to fear. He knew that Belgium as a country was neutral; he knew that Germany and Austria would never overrun a neutral country. "You can hang me from this lamppost if the Germans march in here," he cried to his friends. They remained skeptical, and their faces turned grimmer as the days went by.

Where had his Belgium gone so suddenly? His supposed land of vitality, of strength, of energy, and the intensity of another kind of life. That was what he so loved about this country and this sea. And why he so admired the country's greatest poet.

Émile Verhaeren had been the first spiritual love of Zweig's life. As a young man, he'd found in him his first object of unconditional admiration. Verhaeren's poems shook Stefan Zweig to the very marrow, as nothing had done before. Verhaeren's was the style against which he honed his own, first imitating it, then making his own free renderings, then translating Verhaeren's work into German, poem by poem. He was the one who had made Émile Verhaeren a name in Germany and Austria, and he had published an effusive appreciation in book form at Insel Verlag in 1913. In it he wrote, "And thus it is time today to speak of Émile Verhaeren, the greatest and indeed perhaps the only Modernist to have absorbed the conscious feeling of contemporary life in poetic terms and bodied it forth, the first to have fixed our era in permanent poetic form with incomparable inspiration and incomparable artistry."

It was also as a result of Verhaeren's inspiration, his joy in life itself, and his trust in the world that Stefan Zweig had traveled to Belgium at the end of June, and to the sea. To strengthen the inspiration he drew from Verhaeren's own inspiration. And to see the man whose poetry he had rendered into German. Like, for example, "Fervor," which begins:

If we truly admire one another
From the very depths of our ardor and our faith,
You the thinkers, you the scholars, you the apostles
You will draw on us to shape the laws that govern this
new world.

They are hymns to life, dream landscapes. Long, clear gazes at the world until it gives off its own illumination and corresponds to the poem that lauds it. And this love of the world, this enthusiasm were both hard-won. Laboriously wrested from a dark reality.

I love my fevered eyes, my brain, my nerves
The blood that feeds my heart, the heart that feeds my
body;

I love mankind and the world, I adore the force
That my forces marshal and receive from man and
    universe

For life's meaning is: Receive and Squander.
My peers are those who exult as I do,
avid, panting in the presence of life's intensity and the
    red fires of its wisdom.

Two untamed creatures from the wilds of yearning had found each other. The young Austrian was enraptured by his conversations with his effusive master.

The assassination of the heir to the Austrian throne had not made him change his plans at all. His secure world seemed secure for all time. Stefan Zweig had experienced more than one crisis, and this one was no different from all the others. It would pass and leave no trace. Like everything in his life thus far.

They were actually due to meet on August 2, but then they crossed paths before that anyway, quite by chance, when Zweig was sitting for the painter Constant Montald in his studio in Brussels, and Verhaeren happened to drop by. They greeted each other and talked with their customary warmth. Zweig's outpouring of enthusiasm struck the bearded Belgian as a little disturbing, but he put up with it. They wanted to see each other again soon and to plunge into discussions about everything imaginable, new poems, new plays, about love too, and new women. Zweig's theme.

But before this, given the young Austrian's excitement, Verhaeren had a proposal: could Zweig meet a friend of his up there in Ostend? A rather strange friend, Verhaeren had to admit. Happy to have himself photographed playing the flute on the roofs of his hometown, a painter too, also made masks and drew caricatures, none too successfully up till now, actually not successfully at all. His first exhibition was held in a friend's carpet shop. Once a year he organized a masked ball and ran all around the town with his friends in full costume. Called it "the Dead Rats' Ball." More people came every year. This man was called James Ensor. Verhaeren gave Zweig the address and a letter of introduction.

And Zweig went. To the shop owned by Ensor's mother, right behind the promenade along the beach. She sold carnival masks and shells and paintings by sailors and dried starfish. A narrow house with big display windows at street level, which showed off the exotic offerings hanging from transparent threads. Zweig went in. Yes, he was told, her son was upstairs, why didn't he just go up? A dark, narrow hallway and stairs carpeted in red, with maliciously smirking masks lining the stairwell. He passed a tiny kitchen, red-enameled pots on the stove, dripping faucet. Up on the third floor a man wearing a flat cap was sitting at the piano playing quietly to himself, apparently oblivious to everything around him. On the wall behind the piano hung an enormous painting; hundreds of people in the strangest masks crowded the canvas, struggling toward some unidentifiable destination. Their stylized faces were in an array of garish colors, with long noses and empty eyes. A ball for the dead, a mortal folk festival, a communal frenzy. Zweig stared, mesmerized. This was not his Belgium. This was the home of Death, this was where he was celebrated. A round table displayed a large armful of dusty grasses in a vase, painted, Chinese, acting as the base for a laughing, toothless skull, wearing a woman's hat stuck with dried flowers. The man at the piano kept playing to himself and humming. Stefan Zweig stood for a while as if paralyzed, then he turned around and ran down the stairs, through the shell shop and onto the sunny street, back into the daylight. He wanted to get away from here, back to being carefree, have something to eat, regain his composure.

He hurried to his companion. Her name was Marcelle, and she had accompanied him here. A fantastic woman. Not marriage material, heavens no, more a novelistic thing. A story one could write up later. A sudden, unexpected intensity in one's life, a plunge, an upward leap. A stunning eruption of passion. A Stefan Zweig story. Lived out, in order to be described.

His first love, Friderike von Winternitz, had stayed at home in Austria. She made no claims on him, nor could she, because she was married to someone else. And so she wrote to Zweig in Ostend to say he should enjoy himself with his little girlfriend, and enjoy the summer. The glorious summer of 1914, to which Stefan Zweig would always think back in later years, when he uttered the word *summer*. The two women, the sun, the sea, the kites in the air, vacationing bathers from all around the world, the great poet, a beach slowly emptying of people.

The German visitors were the first to leave, followed by the English. Zweig stayed on. His excitement grew. On the twenty-eighth of July, Austria declared war on Serbia, and troops were marshaled on the border with Russia. Now even Stefan Zweig was slowly obliged to realize that things could turn serious. He bought himself a ticket for the Ostend Express on the thirtieth of July. It was the last train to leave Belgium for Germany that summer.

Every carriage was jammed, people were standing in the corridors. Everyone had a different rumor to recount, and every rumor was believed. When the train was approaching the German border and suddenly stopped in open country, and Stefan Zweig saw huge trucks coming toward them, all covered with tarpaulins, and thought he recognized the shapes of cannons underneath, it gradually dawned on him where this train was headed. It was headed into war, which now was ineluctable.

Stefan Zweig went into a frenzy. He wrote down everything, at once, in an exact but racing torrent in his diary, which he began to keep again. He could no longer sleep, he was unsteady on his feet, he wrote, "I am totally broken, I can't eat, every nerve is twitching." He felt ashamed in front of his friends when he hadn't yet been called up by the third of August. Even Hofmannsthal* had already been called up. Most of all, he felt ashamed in front of women. He felt their looks. What are you still doing here, young man? they seemed to be asking. He himself didn't know either.

He did military service at home at his desk, writing an account for the newspaper of his return journey into war and justified himself in his diary by writing that only the very last lines of his article were something of a lie. "Never has Vienna seemed so lovable to me," he wrote for the newspaper, "and I rejoice that this was the very hour in which I found my way back to her." In his diary, on the other hand: "Vienna was in a state of consternation when I reached there on the 31st of July. People stood around the call-up placards for hours on end, struggling to under-

*The poet and playwright Hugo von Hofmannsthal.

stand their incomprehensibly abysmal German. As evening came, some of them (mostly veterans' associations) tried to evince some enthusiasm, but it sounded pretty subdued."

Little lies. It was war. Truth was dead.

Nonetheless Zweig believed every word he read in the German and Austrian newspapers: poisoned wells in Germany, helpless Germans stood against walls and shot. And then, on the fourth of August, a piece of news that struck him like a bolt of lightning. GERMANY INVADES BELGIUM! Was this folly or genius? He couldn't believe it would go well. Germany and Austria were pitted against the whole world. Above all, Stefan Zweig wanted to go to sleep for six months, in order not to witness this defeat. His whole body shook. Not because of his friends in Belgium, not because of the little neutral country into which the German army had marched, the quicker to reach Paris. Not because of his Belgium, that glorious country with its vitality, its mixture of peoples, its joie de vivre, its enjoyment of the pleasures of life, that he'd celebrated before in his book on Verhaeren as the embodiment of the true Europe, and that had heroically resisted all invaders over the centuries. "At that time all they wanted was to preserve their bright and merry way of life, with its untrammeled Dionysian appetites, an empire of sensuous indulgence; they wanted to preserve their excesses as mere moderation."

His Belgium (which didn't have much to do with the real Belgium). He'd given up. Zweig now trembled only for Germany. And for Austria.

He raced through the streets of Vienna in pursuit of the latest news, of new rumors, new announcements of victories by the German army. If word came suddenly that the war ministry was about to announce a great victory, he rushed there in the company of thousands of his fellow Viennese. They buzzed around the brightly lit windows like insects in the night. And again, no victory. Again another night without sleep.

Stefan Zweig wanted to get out onto the field of battle. He grew a beard, so that he would look determined, wild, and ready to fight. The day Germany invaded Belgium, he made a will. He withdrew a large sum of money out of the safe at his bank. His diary entry reads: "The German victories are glorious!" He was in a fever. He cheered. He wrote, "Free air at last!" And how he envied Berlin its celebrations.

Even years later, long after he's become a world-famous pacifist and has lived through other cataclysms, he writes in his memoir *The World of Yesterday* that despite all his abhorrence, despite his hatred of war, he would never want to have missed those days in August. Everything was smashed in the course of those days. Eternally, irreparably.

And yet it was an extraordinary moment. "As never before, thousands upon hundreds of thousands felt what it would have been far better they had felt in peacetime: that they were as one."

Zweig wrote adoring letters to Ida Dehmel, the wife of Richard Dehmel, the most rabid warmonger among the German poets, who from the very first days of the war had distinguished himself not just in the field but at his desk with the most fiery, nationalistic, fighting verse. "Even were the great and eternal efforts of our nation to end in the destruction of the state itself," Zweig wrote to Frau Dehmel, "these poems alone would leave us thankful for our danger and our inner affliction."

What a misfortune that the other side retaliated with its own poems. It was the ninth of November when Zweig made a diary entry about "a small catastrophe in my existence." For his teacher, his father, his model, his great Belgian friend Verhaeren had also been writing poetry. German and Austrian newspapers printed his verses as a demonstration of sheer monstrosity. They were the first poems by the Belgian that had not been translated by Stefan Zweig. Zweig had learned early on about Verhaeren's intention to write about the war, and he had burdened their common friend Romain Rolland with the task of urging him "to commit only those things to verse, and hence to posterity, that he knew for certain were true." But Verhaeren turned every horror story about German atrocities into lyrical truths. Virgins raped, women's breasts hacked off, children's feet severed and carried in the pockets of German soldiers. All of it in the poetic voice of the bard of life, drunk on images, that Zweig so worshiped.

> O *tragic sun made witness in Flanders*
> *Of women in flames and cities in ashes*
> *Of long-drawn-out horror and sudden crime*
> *For which German sadism hungered and thirsted.*

Stefan Zweig was bewildered: to whom had he given all his love and worshipful admiration? These lines were written by the same man who had symbolized the best of Europe to him, and who had taught him "that only a perfect man can be a good poet." In despair, Zweig asked himself if maybe everything had been false—the very fundament of his life, translating and writing poetry.

The worst aspect of this poem about Belgium was the accusation of barbarity, the assertion that this German war was being prosecuted by means that were not all honorable or civilized. The war as Stefan Zweig imagined it was heroism and willingness to sacrifice for an end both worthy and necessary. And the enemy too should demonstrate good behavior. "My greatest good fortune as an officer would be to ride out against a civilized foe," he wrote, he, the son of a textile manufacturer from Vienna, to his publisher Kippenberg in Germany. Zweig had very romantic notions about war. An amateur gentleman rider with exquisite manners and a saber, in the saddle against civilized opponents, for example the French.

In these months he envied the Germans not just their victories but, most of all, their enemies. Zweig didn't want to fight against Russia, he didn't want to fight barbarians, Slavs, and the enemies of civilization. In the letter to his German publisher, he spelled out the details of those *for* whom he had little desire to fight either: Those outposts of the Danube monarchy that were the most threatened in the first months of the war. The regions close to the Russian border where people spoke Polish, Russian, or Yiddish. The unknown, distant, rather sinister territories of the East. Zweig wrote to Kippenberg, "This may explain to you why not one of Austria's intellectuals has willingly volunteered for the front, and why those who were obliged by their status to do so even arranged for themselves to be transferred out again—we lack any connection, as you must well understand. Brody does not signify to me what Insterburg does; the first left me cool, the second caused me to tremble when I learned it had been laid waste! Finally there is only one supreme connection; language is our only home."

...

YES, BRODY LEFT Stefan Zweig unmoved. He had never so much as been to the place. There was hardly a person in the Vienna of those years who knew Brody, the little town in Galicia at the far edge of the Danube monarchy. And if anyone did know it, then it was as the synonym for poverty, the home of poor Orthodox eastern Jews, the embarrassing distant kin of the assimilated western Jews in Vienna. Brody was far away. In Vienna no one wanted to fight for Brody, certainly not any intellectuals, and most certainly not Stefan Zweig.

Not even twenty thousand people lived at that time in the little border town that from the very outbreak of war found itself at the center of the first slaughter. Three-quarters of the population were Jews. For many years Brody had been a well-to-do market town, the meeting point of traders from Russia, Poland, and Austria, but since the railroad between Odessa and Lemberg had been opened in 1879 and no longer stopped in Brody, the town had been cut off and forgotten. A young writer would later recall the town as follows: "Everything was peaceful at home. The only enmities were between closest neighbors. People got drunk but then made their peace. Business rivals did one another no harm. They took it out on customers and buyers instead. Everyone lent everyone else money. Everyone owed everyone else money. Nobody had anything to reproach anyone else with.

"Political parties were not tolerated. No one made distinctions between people of different nationalities, because everyone spoke everyone else's languages. Jews were identifiable only by their traditional clothes and their hauteur. Sometimes there were little pogroms, but in the general whirl of events, they were soon forgotten. The dead Jews were buried, and those who had been robbed lied about having suffered damages."

This writer was an ambitious, talented Jew with short, dark hair, slightly prominent ears, very blue eyes, and a look of permanent skepticism. And he did everything in his power to leave Brody as soon as he could.

He was very good at school. He liked to reinforce his statements with an emphatic "That's a fact"; as he called himself Muniu, this soon earned him the friendly nickname of Muniufact. He had grown up with his mother in the household of his grandfather Jechiel Gruebel, who lodged with the rich uniform tailor Kalman Ballon in the Goldgasse. He had never met his father, who had left on a business trip, or so he was told, before his son was born, and had not come back. Supposedly he had gone mad. Or alcohol had addled his mind and killed him.

Muniu's real name was Joseph Roth. In 1913 he made it to the university in Lemberg, the capital of Galicia, and in another six months he succeeded in pushing on to Vienna. He was enraptured and intimidated by the scale and the brilliance of the imperial capital. One of his first walks took him to the apartment house of an admired writer whom he wanted to thank for his books, to whom he wanted to express his adulation, whom he wanted to catch even a glimpse of, or at least see where he lived. So there, in 1913, stood Joseph Roth in front of Stefan Zweig's apartment. He waited for a while outside the closed front door, and then, having not seen his idol, he went home.

. . .

In the summer of 1914 Joseph Roth was home in Galicia for the vacation, in Brody and in Lemberg. When the news of the assassination of the Austrian crown prince reached him, he was sitting with his friend Soma Morgenstern, talking about their studies and talking about Vienna. They sensed that war was on the way, and to them, war meant war against Russia. And in turn: victory over Russia. They longed for Russia's defeat. They had still been children when Russia lost the war against Japan in 1905. Even back then they were thrilled. It would happen again, they knew it for sure. But none of it had much to do with them personally.

They made jokes about the imminent war, and they went to a Jewish inn, the best in Lemberg according to Roth, called Zehngut. The fatherless Roth wanted to know everything about Soma Morgenstern's father. How much he loved him, how much he wanted his son to study law, and so on. A very old man, a regular guest, with a pointed beard, came into the inn. Roth looked at him, fascinated. How would Morgenstern himself look when he was old? he asked his friend. Morgenstern had never thought about it. And anyway, the men in his family didn't live to such an age. But Roth had thought about it long and hard. He would live to be very old, he was certain. He explained this to his startled friend: "And this is how I always see myself: I'm a skinny old man. I wear a long black robe with long sleeves that almost cover my hands. It's fall, and I take walks in a garden and think up devious plots against my enemies. Against my enemies and my friends too." It was the first time he'd told Soma any of this, but it's a story he'd tell in future again and again. Himself as an old man, with his long sleeves and his devious plots.

After the war broke out, Morgenstern and Roth met again, this time in Vienna. The headline in the *Neue Freie Presse* was LEMBERG STILL IN OUR POSSESSION! It became their standard greeting, even long after Austria lost Lemberg, just like Brody and the entire great empire. The world of yesterday.

. . .

At the same time Stefan Zweig was sitting surrounded by his friends at the seaside, laughing at the world until suddenly he was at the edge of the abyss and in desperate urgency got on the last train home. A wild departure, back into the flatlands, both abrupt and unexpected for someone who, like Hans Castorp, had failed to read the newspapers or, when he finally did read them, had failed to take them seriously.

Many years later Zweig thinks back with longing to this summer in his life. "When every man was called up, to hurl his petty self into the furnace of the masses, in order to purge himself of all self-regard. All differences of status, of language, of class, of religion were inundated in this one moment by the floodtide of brotherly love. Strangers spoke to one another on the street, people who had avoided one another for years shook one another's hands, one saw lively faces everywhere. Each individual experienced a heightening of earlier times, he was now absorbed into the general mass, he was 'the people,' and his person, his otherwise ignored person, had acquired a meaning."

. . .

IT IS JULY AGAIN. A new summer in Ostend.

The streetlamps from which Stefan Zweig said he would hang himself are still there. And the sea is the same too, the expansive long beach, the big, overly broad promenade, the elaborately curved casino with its large terrace, the bistros with their little marble tables outside, the wooden bathing huts in the sand. The newspapers lie on the bistro tables, but there are no newsboys calling out alarming headlines for the Austrian tourists to make fun of. The mood along the shore is boisterous, the season has just begun, it's hot, the entire youth of Belgium seems to have gathered this summer in what the advertising brochures like to call "Queen of Beach Resorts," on the white spun-sugar promenade by the North Sea. July 1936, in Ostend.

Stefan Zweig thinks back to that last innocence, remembering a world he believed to be eternal, a world without end, and a man in a flat cap in a kingdom of the dead in mass revolt, a boneyard of masks.

But Ostend also conjures up memories of bursts of

energy, and intensity and strength, of a new beginning with the force of a catapult, ripping him out of contented inertia to encounter the utterly unexpected possibility of a new world and its equally unanticipated sense of spiritual brotherhood. So even after the cataclysmic destruction began, with its aftershocks still to be felt now, in this new summer, the place itself would forever be associated with the hope of a sudden change in the course of the universe. What a youthful, yearning young man, so susceptible to wild enthusiasm, Stefan Zweig had been in 1914!

Twenty-two years have passed since that summer, years in which he has become a world star of literature. His name is as internationally famous as that of Thomas Mann, his books outsell those of any other German author around the world. His novellas, his historical biographies, and *Shooting Stars* are global best sellers. He's a child of Fortune, owns a little yellow castle in the woods up on the Kapuzinerberg overlooking Salzburg, corresponds with every great mind on the Continent, and has long been married to his love of those years back then, Friderike von Winternitz. And now, in this new summer, he is a man struggling to find a foothold.

Zweig has barely ever bothered with present-day politics or religion in the world in which he lives. In history— yes! If it was the world of Mary Queen of Scots, Marie

Antoinette, or Joseph Fouché, he knew every historical and political detail, the mechanisms of power, the world-historical context, all of which he encompassed in his books as part of the human story, the story of mighty, individual people. Or, occasionally, as the story of powerless people who were singled out by a world-historical lightning bolt to change the course of destiny. None of it had anything to do with the world he actually lived in.

It is only in recent years that he has begun to sketch himself in his historical personages and his present world in historical events.

Two years ago he published a book about the humanist Erasmus of Rotterdam, and most recently a monograph titled *Castellio Against Calvin*, which carried as its subtitle *A Conscience Against Power*. Erasmus and Castellio are the heroes in whom he also describes himself, the ideals for which he strives: conscience against power, humanism, cosmopolitanism, tolerance, and reason. In the life and teachings of Erasmus, Zweig discerns the art of ameliorating conflicts by "well-intentioned understanding" and "the absolute will to comprehend" per se. In Calvin's opponent Castellio he sees the great anti-ideologue who despised terror and intolerance and fought against them with his pen until, exhausted by the long struggle, he died without achieving victory. That Zweig, with his pleas for tolerance and understanding, has recently been reaping a harvest of intolerance and incomprehension, in émigré circles first and foremost, is something he finds utterly bewildering.

But these are the years when decisions must be made, the years of resolution. Zweig is still writing out of a world, and about a world, that no longer exists. His ideal is pointless, unrealistic, risible, and dangerous. His analogies no longer have a place in a present in which the enemy holds all the power. What use is tolerance in a world in which any man and everything he lives for and everything he writes are in danger of being ground to a pulp?

"Fight or shut up," Joseph Roth wrote to him. But Zweig doesn't want to fight. He wants to keep quiet in the first years after the Nazis seize power in Germany. Even after his books are burned on the Opernplatz in Berlin. Quiet—the better to keep working and living in peace. And perhaps the better to ensure that his books continue to be sold in Germany and he can continue to influence his readers there. For a time this even seems to work. In the first years of Nazi rule in Germany, Zweig's books are still available to German readers.

This finally comes to an end in the summer of 1936. His German publisher Anton Kippenberg is no longer allowed to issue his books, yet Zweig still doesn't switch to one of the German-language publishers in exile like Querido or Allert de Lange, which are based in Amsterdam. He goes to the little Austrian publishing house of Herbert Reichner, who, although he is a Jew, is still able to get his books shipped into Germany and thus is excoriated by many émigrés, including Roth, as Hitler's house Jew who's prepared to make any compromise just to keep doing business with Germany. To Zweig, Reichner is still a fragment of Austria, a connection to his old homeland. He himself is barely ever there anymore. Since his house on the Kapuzinerberg was searched by police in February 1934, who were on the hunt for the cache of weapons of the Workers' Republican Defense Alliance, it's been lost territory to him. This experience was not only an insult to his writings and his work, which for so many years has been dedicated to nonviolence—it was an intrusion by the state into his very world, and the protected realm of his creative output.

The house is now nothing more than a burden, a memory, a museum of his earlier life. Even when he lived there, it had had something of the aura of a museum. Zweig was a collector of antiquities, particularly of written artifacts: manuscripts, leaves of notebooks. He owned manuscripts by Balzac and Maupassant, Nietzsche, Tolstoy, Dostoyevsky, Goethe, Gustav Mahler, Mozart, and almost every contemporary writer. He had begged each of them for a sheet of paper, one story; he owned the manuscript of Heinrich Mann's *The Road to Hell*, Hermann Hesse's novella *Heumond*, Arthur Schnitzler's *Call to Life*, poems by Oscar Wilde and Walt Whitman, Richard Dehmel, Paul Claudel, and Hugo von Hofmannsthal, plays by Wedekind and Hauptmann, and Rainer Maria Rilke's *The Lay of the Love and Death of Christoph Cornet Rilke*, which begins:

> *Riding, riding, riding, through the day, through the*
> *   night, through the day.*
> *Riding, riding, riding.*
> *And the heart has become so tired, and the longing so*
> *   vast. There are no longer any hills; hardly a tree.*
> *   Nothing dares to rise up. Alien huts squat, thirsting,*
> *   beside muddy wells. Nowhere a tower. And always*
> *   the same scene. One has two eyes too many.*

These things that were important to Stefan Zweig in the worlds of the intellect, of literature, and of music, he possessed in the handwriting of those who had created them. They are relics of the world in which he feels at home, in which he lives and whose existence he renews in his writing. He is a great admirer, a selfless worshiper of the art of others. This art, European culture, is his religion.

His altar is Ludwig van Beethoven's desk, at which he loves to sit and which he took with him to London, where Friderike set up a new apartment for him at the beginning of the year. Yes, he kept the desk, a page from Goethe's *Faust*, and the latter's poem about the violet annotated by Mozart. It's the terrible, masochism-saturated opposite piece to the romantic "Little Wild Rose," and it ends:

Alas! Alas! The girl went past:
Unseen the violet in the grass was crushed, poor violet.
It drooped and died, and yet it cried:
"And though I die, yet still I die
By her, by her,
By her feet passing by."

He parted company with the rest of the collection, selling it to the autograph dealer Martin Bodmer in Zurich.

In 1925 Stefan Zweig had written a novella about a blind old man who had once possessed one of the most astonishing collections of engravings and drawings in the world and now sits, sightless and impoverished, among his family in inflation-ravaged Germany, still proud of his works on paper, his entire estate. Each day he has them laid out in front of him, one by one. But his unfortunate family, in sheer desperation, has long since sold the collection. The old man has no idea. An art dealer comes to visit from Berlin; the family begs him not to betray them. So the blind collector shows the stranger his pride and joy. Every sheet of paper is blank, substituted by the family as each piece was sold. The blind man is oblivious; his pride and his certainty that all this is his have remained untouched all through the years. "And thus this triumphant cascade of words continued for two whole hours. I cannot tell you how eerie it was to be with him as we looked at these hundred or two hundred blank scraps of paper, that were so unbelievably real to this tragic, innocent man that he described and praised every one of them in their exact order, without a single error. The invisible collection, which must have been scattered to the four winds long since, was so unmistakably present for this blind, heart-breakingly deceived man, and his passionate vision was so overwhelming, that even I began to believe in its reality."

Now it is Zweig's collection that is being scattered to the winds. He knows that years of wandering lie ahead, and that the new apartment in London will not become a new home. He wants to be free, or a little free, in this world of bonds and shackles.

. . .

Nineteen thirty-six is a year of farewells and decisions for Stefan Zweig. His German publishing house no longer publishes him, the German market is lost to him, along with Austria, his collection, and his magnificent house— all of it is now nothing but a wearying burden. It is not easy to jettison what one has built up over the years. An entire life. Will a new one begin? Everything old is a fetter. Most of all his wife, Friderike, who back in 1914, when she was still in her first marriage, had sent word to Ostend to "have lots of fun with Marcelle"; Friderike, whom he had married in 1920.

Stefan Zweig doesn't want this marriage anymore. Love is long gone.

It was two years ago that Friderike surprised him in Nice with his secretary, Lotte Altmann. A painful situation for everyone involved, but Friderike was prepared to draw a veil of silence over it all. She knew her husband, she knew his books, his novellas about passion. She knew what was to be expected, it was part of his life. And now she had just caught him at it for the first time. Friderike Zweig didn't consider Lotte Altmann to be a real rival.

Later Friderike was keen to tell everyone who wanted to know, and everyone else as well, that it was she who had chosen Lotte Altmann as her husband's secretary. Diligent, quiet, pale, sickly, unobtrusive, gifted at languages. These were the qualities that had struck Friderike and that in her eyes had made Lotte the ideal secretarial help for the duration of Stefan Zweig's stay in England.

Lotte Altmann, born in Kattowitz in Upper Silesia in 1908, had studied French, English, and economics at the University of Frankfurt. As a Jew, she had already been denied formal status in the summer of 1933. Her brother was a doctor and since May 1933 had already been banned from practicing. He and his whole family had soon decided to look on this as a kind of blessing, for it compelled them to leave Germany early, before the great wave of refugees was unleashed. Her brother opened a practice in London that achieved some considerable success; as time passed, more and more German émigrés came to him as patients. Lotte Altmann was attending language courses in the hopes of getting work one day as a librarian, when the job with Stefan Zweig was offered to her in the spring of 1934. A dream for her; she would never have imagined being allowed to work with this world-famous man and even to be of assistance to him in many situations. She was twenty-six years old when she met him, unsure of herself, without a profession or a husband or a country. And a dream for him too, very uneasy in this foreign city and in the English language, and so more in need of support than he had ever been. He was fifty-three and world famous. Famous, yes, but shy and strangely ill at ease in new situations and in company, never entirely sure of himself. Stefan Zweig was a seeker, always trying to locate the still center in himself, always pursuing self-awareness. A man who always admired others for their secure footing in the world. He, by contrast, was constantly summoning all his strength to stand steady without examining himself constantly to check that this stance was good and upright and respectable and proper and stable. For a man like him, a threatened state of exile was fatal. Riches and fame were of no help to him. He was totally dependent on his homeland and the security it offered him, and on his friends. And he was worried about getting older. One of the darkest days of his life had been his fiftieth birthday. He couldn't tolerate aging. And then into his life came this pale, beautiful, young, reserved, intelligent woman who worshiped him silently, admired his writing, and loved his shy ways. It was that very shyness that Friderike had tolerated at best, that she regarded as a silly, somewhat embarrassing affectation even after all their years of marriage. At some point it would happen, she thought, at some point his fame and social routine would cure him of it. But it didn't get better; on the contrary, the older he got, the worse his insecurity became, and the more acute his self-scrutiny, his unsteadiness, his fear of any gust of wind and of anything unknown.

Lotte was a known quantity to him from the very first, without a word being said. Her quietness, her childlike joy in little things, her attentiveness when she looked at him and asked him things that no one had asked him for years, about his work and his books, things that Friderike and his daughters had long taken for granted about him.

And he didn't need to instruct her as to his literary intentions. All she had to do was to write his letters, ensure that there were always enough stamps, that bills got paid and appointments were kept. But she wanted to know everything, not in a demanding way but with a look that made him talk and talk. What he wrote had a significance. None of it was routine to her, or the obligations of the job. Through her eyes he recaptured his own vision of why he wrote, and the purpose of his labors, the fussing over every comma, his designs for a new world. Just the way Roth had once written to him in his wonderfully exaggerated fashion to say that it didn't matter a shit if millions of Russians were learning the alphabet, the only thing that mattered was that someone called Stefan Zweig was writing. That was it. So none of it was in vain, none of it was some mere fulfillment of an obligation that, once in finished book form, would be attacked in every literary, political, and moral aspect by the critics and thrown to the winds. It was important, it was the creation of another world. This was what Roth kept telling him in his letters. And this was what Lotte Altmann said to him unbidden. It came from inside her. And Stefan Zweig loved her for it, with a silent, restrained, shy depth of feeling. "A young woman loves me," he had written to Roth. And when he was away from her, what he wrote to her in his somewhat old-fashioned, hesitant way was "I wish you might miss me a little." And that he worried about her, since she seemed to care so little about her own happiness. He wanted her always to know how much he himself cared about her happiness, and there was no way she could know this, but he was loyal, a faithful man when once he encountered true friendship. He never forgot. In this he was different from other men, he wrote, and would never forget her or what she was giving him. She could depend on this, she must depend on it, forever.

When he went to Scotland to research his biography of Mary Queen of Scots, he took her with him. As his secretary, to write down what he dictated, but most of all as observer, as interlocutor, as an enraptured young woman who was so eager to learn everything about the life of this queen, what it had really been like, how one might view it from today's perspective, how Stefan Zweig saw it, how she saw it through his eyes.

For a long time Friderike Zweig guessed none of this. She was too convinced she knew her husband, and she despised pale Lotte too much. She was overconfident that her life as Frau Zweig would continue forever as it had until now. So she passed over this little episode. But her husband did not. Not that he articulated this; she had to piece it together from hints and tales told to her by friends.

With the passage of time she was obliged to admit that something was irreparably broken. He had distanced himself from Austria and the yellow house, and now he was distancing himself from her too.

Friderike is very attached to the house in Salzburg; she identifies with its scale and its grandeur. And she doesn't understand her husband's revulsion at the police search, or at least she doesn't share it. She can go on living there quite happily with her two grown daughters.

That's all Zweig needs. He only has to hear mention of the two daughters, and he goes into a rage: dependent, needy, vain, useless—the chains that weigh down his life. The refrain runs through his letters. But the heaviest burden is their mother.

The last time she was in London, they had had only written communication with each other. He made a list of the times when she was forbidden to enter the apartment. He needed peace and quiet. She didn't stick to it. He was furious. She was persistent. He was evasiveness itself, hated conflict, particularly a conflict like this, when everything depended on it. "You are utterly heartless," she said in a letter, as she left London after a huge fight, on her way back to Salzburg.

Friderike has no more than a suspicion that Zweig and Lotte Altmann are now a couple. Before her departure in May, she happened to go into a restaurant where he was sitting with Lotte. "An awkward encounter" was how she put it in a letter to her husband. In her correspondence with Stefan Zweig, she only ever referred to Lotte Altmann as "A" or, in ironic quotation marks, as "your close friend." To friends, she speaks of her as the "Viper."

· · ·

Stefan Zweig flees through the world, striking off one fetter after the other, if possible without causing anyone pain. It's an illusion. The fetters only tighten.

And the new book is no source of joy. Of all places, the protests start in unoccupied Switzerland. May was when there were anniversary celebrations of the Reformation in Geneva and other Swiss cities. Calvin was honored as a national saint. And he was the man whom Zweig in his book made into a forerunner of Hitler. His friend the Communist Romain Rolland sent effusive congratulations from Villeneuve in Switzerland. "Your book is perfectly timed for the four hundredth anniversary of the Reformation. I don't advise you to settle here anytime soon. Beware the fury of the so-called 'Momiers.' When the French edition comes out, you'll be torn to pieces. They'll never forgive you for your attack on Calvin."

The aggressive, battle-hardened, eminently political Nobel Prize–winner Rolland meant his congratulations seriously. He had encouraged Zweig repeatedly to go on the attack, and he seemed barely able to believe that his friend had so determinedly set out to follow him. But this letter filled Zweig with horror. It hadn't been his intention. Was he once again going to reap nothing but hate for a book in which he was celebrating the gentle, flexible, restrained Castellio as his hero? For this the French were going to tear him to pieces?

Him, Zweig, the herald of balance, of listening, of communication? But that was how things were in this world, in this year, on this continent. Moreover, he had yielded to the pressure from his publisher Reichner to finish the book in such haste that several historical errors were not caught in the first printing. A further joy for his enemies. The attacks didn't let up.

Stefan Zweig was having a severe life crisis. He was tired, irritable, and depressed. He was sick of literature, he wrote. What he'd really like to do would be to buy up the entire print run of *Calvin* and burn it. "The only way to fight hatred must come from ourselves," he replied to Rolland. He was dreaming, he said, of retreating into a mousehole and, most of all, of never having to read a newspaper again. The universe, literature, politics—wouldn't it be wonderful never to have to think about them again? Where would be the farthest place from it all? Where would he find the mousehole for this summer?

A beach in Belgium, white house, sun, a broad promenade, little bistros looking out over the water. He wants Ostend.

With Lotte.

"Dear Fraülein Altmann," he writes from Vienna to London on June 22. They're going to spend July together in Ostend, and they're going to be setting off in a week.

"Large suitcases unnecessary," he writes. "We're going to live simply."

...

THIS SUMMER THAT OTHER MAN, the man from Brody in the far east of the empire, is living right nearby. For a few months he has left Paris for Amsterdam, and at the end of May he writes to Stefan Zweig, "You must realize that everyone everywhere has a relative, a mother, a brother, a cousin, but I come from a very long way away, and I don't even know the names of my relatives in the east anymore. And if they are still alive, they're certainly living in absolute penury. What am I to do? I have to treat you as my brother, I beg you, allow me to speak to you just like a brother."

Joseph Roth has reached the end. By comparison with him, Stefan Zweig's problems are in the realm of luxury. Immediately after the Nazis took power in Germany, Roth's books were banned. Nor does he want them to be available there anymore. "Hell reigns," he writes to Zweig. He also says there can be no compromises with the enemy. Anyone who continues to have business in Germany, anyone who so much as maintains any connection to Germany, is a monster. He regards Zweig's decision to keep his books on sale in Germany via the Reichner publishing operation as a betrayal. In May 1936, after it has become clear that Zweig's books will no longer be able to be sold there either, a jubilant Roth writes: "I congratulate you on being banned in Germany."

· · ·

These two men have been bound for years by a remarkable love. Zweig, the elder by thirteen years, owner of a castle, man of the world, best-selling author—and Roth, successful journalist, feature writer in the 1920s for the *Frankfurter Zeitung*, author of not-very-successful documentary novels, inhabiter of hotel rooms, drinker, gregarious, generous, garrulous, always surrounded by friends, audiences, and hangers-on. When finally he wrote *Job* and *Radetsky March*, novels that would in any rational world have brought him both fame and fortune, his books were banned and burned, and he went into exile.

He is an unhappy man, clear-sighted and angry, and he seeks salvation in the past, in old Austria and its monarchy, its empire, that took him, the fatherless Jew who grew up so far from the great, glittering capital and raised him up and opened the world to him. A state that was a universe, that encompassed many different peoples without distinguishing between them, and in which one could travel freely without a passport or papers of any kind. The older he gets and the more the world darkens, the more he yearns to travel back in time to that other world that is transfigured in his eyes, and is lost.

"Lemberg still in our possession." Now, so many years after it fell and the empire itself collapsed, Lemberg seems more completely his than ever before.

In the spring of 1936, Joseph Roth started on the novel about his homeland. It was supposed to be called *Strawberries*. "In my hometown there lived roughly ten thousand people. Three thousand of them were crazy, if not a danger to the others. A gentle derangement enveloped them like a golden cloud. They pursued their business and earned money. They married and begat children. They read books and newspapers. They spent no time worrying about the affairs of the world. They spoke to one another in every language in which the mingled peoples of our region communicated among themselves."

He would never finish the book. His situation worsened dramatically in the course of three months. He had received advances for several novels, and these were long spent. The exiles' publishing house, always on the verge of bankruptcy, would give him no more money unless and until he delivered a finished book. One novel, *Confession of a Murderer,* was almost completed; another, *Weights and*

Measures, was half done; he wrote and he wrote. He used the material from the *Strawberries* novel to fill out the other books so as to finish them more quickly. He knew this wasn't a good idea. Even Zweig, who had always admired him to a fault, warned him in his letters not to "stuff" his novels. It was what had damaged the last book, he said. But what was Roth to do? He had no money.

From a distance Zweig kept trying to appeal to Roth's good sense, to get him to save money, to drink less, to stop living in the most expensive hotels. At the end of March he wrote, "You should finally have the courage to admit to yourself that no matter how great your stature as a writer, you are in material terms a poor, small Jew, almost as poor as seven million others, and you are going to have to live like nine-tenths of the people on this earth, in the tiniest and narrowest estate." This letter almost put an end to their friendship. Joseph Roth was deeply offended. Zweig had put a name to the root of what divided them, the deep gulf that yawned invisibly between the assimilated western Jew born to wealth and the poor eastern Jew from the far frontier of the monarchy. It was self-defense. For Zweig saw that he couldn't help Roth, that it didn't matter how much money he gave him, that he just kept sinking deeper and deeper into the abyss, because he was drinking more and more heavily, slowly losing his mind and with it his art. "You do not need to tell *me*, of all people, what a little poor Jew is," Roth replied. "I have been one since 1894 and am proud of it. A devout eastern Jew from Radziwillow. Stop it! I've been poor and I've been small for thirty years. *I am poor.*"

Roth cursed, stormed, begged Zweig to come to him. "I'm dying, I'm dying," he wrote. And on the ninth of April: "Dear friend, if you want to come, then come soon, what's left of me will be thrilled." The situation was dramatic, and Roth heightened the drama in the letters to his friend. Zweig dodged. The only flights to Amsterdam were by Lufthansa, and he wasn't going to fly Lufthansa. At the same time he wrote to his American publisher, Ben Huebsch, saying he was afraid of meeting Roth. He'd been telling him for years to rein himself in financially, alcoholically, and literarily. Nothing had helped, and nothing would ever help. "One could wish he would commit some minor infraction that would get him jailed for two or three months. There's no other way to stop him drinking." And he added the information that would be fatal to Roth: "The quality of his books must suffer over the long term because of the folly of his way of life."

Zweig, naturally, is right. But the American market is the only possible financial salvation for German writers, and Huebsch the publisher is powerful.

Zweig wrote to Roth, "Roth, hold yourself together now, we *need* you. There are so few people and so few books in this overpopulated world!" But Roth was still clear-sighted, even now. A good judge of character and an acute reader. He knew that Zweig didn't want to come and didn't want to see him. And he could read flight schedules: "It's not correct that only German planes fly here. The only Lufthansa flight is the 6 a.m. Besides that one there are *Dutch* flights at 7 a.m., 10, 12, 3 p.m., 2:10 p.m., and 7:45. But you simply don't want to come, and you'd do better to say so." And yes, he would hold himself together, Zweig wasn't to worry. He was holding himself together, nobody could hold himself together more than he was doing day by day. "I write every day, if only to lose myself in the fates of strangers. Don't you see, my fellow human, my friend, my brother—you once said Brother in a letter—that I'm close to dying?"

It was an aerial battle being fought in dire straits by the two writers. Aerial chess between friends. Who would give way? Could Zweig save his friend? Did he even want to? The man who wanted to free himself of all shackles was now attached to this particular shackle and couldn't get free. Roth was not prepared to release him from the responsibilities of their friendship. Zweig had a bad conscience and struggled with himself. He did love his friend, he still admired his art, and he respected his judgment more than anyone else's. Roth had always been severe with him, devoid of leniency. The flowery, the cloudy, the metaphorically overflowing, the false images, the adjectives that only half fit—Roth was pitiless, both in his letters and in conversation. He didn't care that he was dependent on Zweig and that the other man was so much more successful than he was. None of it had anything to do with precision, beauty, or literary quality. But he also knew what his own literary debt to Stefan Zweig was. He knew it, and he put it down on paper. In 1930 he dedicated a copy of *Job* to him with these words: "Stefan Zweig, to whom I owe thanks for this *Job*—and more than *Job*, and more than any book—for the full measure of friendship: please accept this book and keep it as a small salute. Joseph Roth."

In 1931 they had written together in Antibes, reading aloud to each other in the evenings what they had written during the day, correcting words, adding words. Roth read to Zweig from what was becoming *Radetsky March*, and Zweig was happy and thrilled and started repeatedly to tell his own stories as he listened, interrupting the reader with memories of his own early Austria, pictures from his childhood.

And later, when Roth sent the finished book to his friend, he included a letter with it: "I totally forgot to tell you that you are the source of some of the scenes in my book. You will recognize them. Despite my dissatisfaction with the novel, I am very, very grateful to you."

Henceforward Stefan Zweig's literary counsel would be almost indispensable to him. In January 1933 Roth wrote to Zweig: "I cannot begin *anything new whatever* until I have talked to you. I have to have your goodness and your intelligence."

. . .

A few weeks later Roth goes through the second half of *Confession of a Murderer* with Zweig once more. He reads aloud, Zweig criticizes, thinks ahead, reformulates, offers ideas, notions, observations, cuts verbiage and repetitions, and points out false connections. Roth listens with fascination and close attention and is open to his suggestions.

In the spring of this year, Roth was totally bowled over for the first time by something his friend had written. The settling of accounts with the reformer, Calvin, was a great joy to Roth, the Jew who revered Catholicism. He read it over three nights, he wrote. "Despite all your worldliness, there was always a lingering impulse toward illusion in your books, or rather an unspoken hope, a certain moral ballast. You've jettisoned that, which has allowed you to reach higher. It's the pristine, the clear, the transparent that I love so much both in the flow of thought *and* in the form itself. The ballast of metaphors has been dropped." And he added, "You can imagine the pleasure this gives me, given my almost Calvinist fanaticism about the purity of language." He continued in this laudatory vein, interrupting himself to say oh he was testing himself to see if his friendly literary conscience would allow him to write this to his patron. But yes, he had examined himself and had nothing to reproach himself with. It was simply too good, and he wasn't being venal. And added, happily, as ultimate praise, "I feel as if you've found your way home, and in a small way that I'm part of it."

One writer finding his way home to another. Joseph Roth was a tactician, Joseph Roth was in despair and wanted at all costs to have his friend by his side. He wanted to talk to him, write with him, drink together, he wanted to be next to him, freed of all worries by this man who paid for everything and solved all problems with his sunny common sense. So his letter was a little exaggerated. But he meant what he said about a homecoming. It was both wish and reality.

Roth felt on the verge of death. His room, he said, looked like a coffin. "Think about how you never know when you're going to see someone for the last time. Letters can't replace that moment when you see each other, greet each other, nor the other, when you say goodbye."

Finally, Stefan Zweig gave in. Roth was part of the reason he decided that Ostend was to be the refuge that summer. His friend could get there quickly by train from Amsterdam; it wasn't far. That there was, moreover, a ban on schnapps in Belgium, as Zweig wrote to tell him delightedly, would not necessarily have been a great attraction to Roth, but he knew his friend's pedagogical ambitions and would find ways to get around them. That it might be a plus that Zweig had chosen a seaside resort was not on Roth's mind either. He liked to say that he didn't set foot in the sea, and fish didn't set foot in cafés. Roth didn't care about a hot sun, he didn't care about beaches, and he didn't care about a happy holiday atmosphere. Zweig appeased him by saying Ostend was a real city, with more of a café culture than Brussels, and more bistros than you could count.

BUT IT'S HARD TO TRAVEL in these times if you're a Jew with an Austrian passport and no means of bribing people, even for the shortest distances, even between the Netherlands and Belgium. Roth has spent two weeks already waiting in Amsterdam for his Belgian visa.

Then things get even more stirred up. Roth too has just separated from his life's companion, Andrea Manga Bell— born in Cameroon, raised in Hamburg, married to a Cameroonian prince—with whom he's been living for the past seven years. She has grown children from her first marriage, a son and a daughter; her husband left them after the birth of the daughter to return to Africa. He apparently possesses a fabulous fortune but pays absolutely nothing to his abandoned wife or the children. Andrea Manga Bell is a former actress who lived out her dream of a royal life in Africa on the stage, then worked as a graphic artist till she met Joseph Roth and took over as his secretary, typing his manuscripts. Since then she has earned no money of her own. So Roth has had to support her. But Roth no longer has the will or the means. He went to Amsterdam in March so as to live more cheaply and get free of the family burden.

In June he writes to his companion and suggests that she come to Amsterdam or later to Brussels, to live with him there. But without the children. It's time they supported themselves, or their father supported them, or whoever. But he, Joseph Roth, is no longer going to do it. If not, they must split up. He receives no reply for a long time. Then on June 28, a telegram arrives from Tueke Manga Bell, Andrea's daughter: "Please come at once!" Nothing else. Roth is in a dreadful state, fearing the worst; he has no money for a trip to Paris, he's been waiting for days in the Hotel Eden for his Belgian visa; he makes a panicked phone call to his French translator Blanche Gidon in Paris. She knows nothing either. Is this comforting in and of itself? Would she have heard if Manga Bell had died? Roth is in despair. For two days he waits for news from Tueke or from Blanche Gidon. Then another telegram from Tueke Manga Bell arrives. Her mother, on learning that Roth intends to part from her, has had a nervous breakdown.

At first Roth is relieved. He had really feared she had taken her own life. A nervous breakdown sounds more like a trick, a fake illness to make him come back to his senses and back to the family. But he's had enough. "Frau Manga Bell has consistently refused to live according to my rules," he writes a few days later to Blanche Gidon to justify himself. He's plagued by guilt, doubly so because the fate of his first great love, Friedl, his wife, lies over him like a shadow. Back then in Berlin, she couldn't live "according to his rules" either, a life of hotels and constant traveling to keep up with her husband. They had lived together only at the very beginning of their marriage in 1922–23, when they shared an apartment in Berlin-Schoeneberg. Then Roth found it burdensome, restricting, somehow false, and they moved from hotel to hotel. Friedl was young, slim, modern, pale, and very pretty. In photos she looked both shy and self-possessed. The marriage made her ill. Roth believes his whole life long that this is his fault. But she was already fragile, nervous, and uneasy in the world when they first met. Roth had written to his cousin Paula Gruebel back then, saying that Friedl "was afraid of people." From Vienna, in the summer of 1922, he wrote, "She spends the day crossing over a ford in the Danube and back again, pretending it's the sea, and lives the life of a creeping plant." And he added, "I would never have believed I could love a little girl this long. I love her shyness in the face of any confession, and the feeling she has which is a mixture of fear and love, and her heart that is always frightened of the very thing she adores."

He saw early on what was happening to her, even if he still swore the opposite in his letters: "She is normal, and

I am what you would have to call mad. She doesn't read the same way I do, not so strongly, not trembling as much, she is less atmospherically predictable, she's straightforward and sensible." In reality, Roth already feared for her sanity in 1925. Four years later he wrote the novel that made him famous, the novel about the pious Jew Mendel Singer, who is tested beyond all measure by God, and whose daughter Miriam loses her mind. In *Job*, Joseph Roth was also describing the fate of his wife. "It is true that you cannot share your pain without doubling it," he wrote in a letter in March 1929. "But this doubling also contains an immeasurable comfort. My suffering moves from the private sphere to the public and thus is easier to endure." Later in the year Friedl suffered such a severe breakdown that she did not recover. Roth described it in a letter to his friend René Schickele in December 1929: "I'm writing to you in desperate need. Yesterday I traveled, indeed I fled to Munich. My wife has been ill since August, psychosis, hysteria, absolute fixation on suicide, she's barely alive—and I'm harried and surrounded by dark red demons, headless, lacking the capacity even to lift a finger, faint and crippled, helpless, with no prospect of getting better." At first Friedl's parents took care of their sick daughter, then the next year, on the same day the last chapter of the *Job* novel was serialized in the *Frankfurter Zeitung*, she was committed to the Rekawinkel sanatorium near Vienna. Later she was moved to the Steinhof psychiatric hospital, also near Vienna.

For the rest of his life, Roth blames himself for Friedl. And so naturally he is horrified when he hears of Manga Bell's nervous breakdown. At the same time he is clearer than ever that he will not go back to her. He has already frequently been afraid of her, always after a fight. Ludwig Marcuse reports later that Roth once begged him urgently to accompany him to a reconciliation with his companion after a long quarrel. She was totally unpredictable, he said, and besides, she always carried a small pistol in her purse. He didn't think it was impossible that she'd use it.

But his fear that Manga Bell may have a psychiatric disorder is almost greater. "I cannot carry the slightest psychic burden anymore without the risk of dying," he writes now to Blanche Gidon. "And I don't want to die."

. . .

One day, after learning of Manga Bell's breakdown, Joseph Roth calls on the Belgian PEN club for help. This finally works, and he gets his visa. But Roth hesitates about making the journey to Ostend. He's discovered that not only Stefan Zweig and Lotte Altmann are there but also Egon Erwin Kisch and Hermann Kesten, fair-weather friends from better days. Roth doesn't feel they're the right company in this dark summer. "I find it truly awkward to meet Kesten and Kisch in Ostend—which is unavoidable," he writes to Zweig. "I can no longer have any patience for jokes."

But Zweig really persuades him, he extols the virtues of Ostend, the hotel prices, and the bistros, and concerning the end of Roth's love affair, which the latter has described to him, he writes cheerfully, "And don't make yourself ill over Ma.Be. It's a stroke of good luck when things suddenly resolve themselves rather than pulling tighter and tighter."

Stefan Zweig knows exactly what he's talking about. Two months previously, at the height of the marital battles in the Zweig household, Joseph Roth had inserted himself cautiously into the argument on the side of Friderike, of whom he was very fond and whose affectionate name for him was Rothi. She had left London more or less in flight. Roth wrote to Zweig, "It's good that your wife has left. I think it's not indiscreet of me to say to you that I advised her to do so. But don't ever forget, dear friend, that she is an exceptionally fine human being and has earned consideration, and that she's at an age when all women fear they're going to be abandoned. It's the age of panic." And he added, "Dear friend, one must love and keep loving, these days. We're all in such a muddle."

Zweig did not reply. Until now, indirectly, as he congratulates him on the sudden end of his love. No comfort for Roth.

In a lecture Roth gave on the twelfth of June to a full house in the bookshop owned by his publisher-in-exile, Allert de Lange, which was titled "Faith and Progress," a much-applauded fulmination against the superstition that modern technology had the power to heal mankind and its very humanity, he ended with the appeal: "Let us set reason in the service of that for which it has been given to us: namely, in the service of love."

And so now: over the border and away from nervous collapse and a love that is over. His visa has come. Up toward the seashore, and a bistro, to meet a friend. A summer of love. July in Ostend.

. . .

He clambers awkwardly out of the train at this, its final stop. Zweig, waiting on the platform, has already made all the arrangements, porter, hotel, the journey from here to there. The reencounter between the two friends up here by the sea is initially a little diffident, stiff, unsure on both sides. For a long time they've communicated only by letter; Roth has given his old friend many angry reproaches and many declarations of love, some exaggerated, some the honest truth. Zweig has dissembled, has avoided meetings, nervous, cautious, concerned to protect his own mental equilibrium. In their letters they have established a competitive, affectionate balance between friendship, envy, admiration, dependency, love, smart-aleck superiority, and mutual jealousy. Roth's despair, alone in Amsterdam, begging for a visa to get to Belgium, has plumbed new depths.

Now they shake hands. "Herr Zweig." "Herr Roth! Finally. Welcome to the sea!" And then everything is back to normal. Roth's relief comes flooding back by the minute. A man, a friend who organizes things for him, his connection to the sun, to common sense, to the guarantee of a safe existence. How gladly he will entrust himself to him this summer. How confident his step becomes immediately. And how happy Zweig is here and now, knowing that he can be the means of good fortune for his friend. How he savors his own superiority. He feels for a moment once again that he's equal to life as he watches his friend walking falteringly along the narrow streets. It's as if they're made for each other. Two men, both falling, but holding each other up for a time.

...

SHE IS EUPHORIC, BEYOND HAPPY, to have got out. Happy that she's escaped from Nazi-land. Irmgard Keun is not Jewish, but her books have been banned in Germany nonetheless. The women she portrayed in *The Artificial Silk Girl* and *Gilgi—One of Us* were far too modern and far too self-aware. Her style is far too modern too, far too redolent of the big city.

She's a self-confident, beautiful young woman, a fur around her neck, a wide mouth, big eyes. And she thought, if anyone was going to start banning books around there, she was going to see about it. So she complained, lodged the complaint with the Nazi authorities, and requested financial assistance for the trial. It's a fact: *Keun v. Propaganda Ministry*. First of all she demanded a valid reason for why her books were no longer to be available, and second, she demanded damages for the confiscated copies. There was more: "The damages I have suffered are in no way limited to my author's share of the confiscated stock; they result from the demonstrable fact that before the books were impounded, my monthly income was several thousand marks, and since they were impounded, it has fallen below one hundred marks." She sent the letter by registered mail to the state court in Berlin. The president of the court passed it on to the Gestapo. From there an inquiry went to the Reichsschrifttumskammer* as to whether Irmgard Keun's writings were actually on the list of noxious and undesirable works. The answer came eight days later and was unambiguous: yes. So Keun got a letter from the Gestapo: "The books were submitted by the president of the Reichsschrifttumskammer pursuant to Article I of the Reichsschrifttumskammer pertaining to noxious and undesirable works, and were confiscated and withdrawn by me. There is no entitlement to compensatory damages." Whereupon Irmgard Keun made claims for compensatory damages to several other state courts, but no legal proceedings were ever opened.

She herself had naturally never expected things to come to trial. But she simply couldn't put up with it. What the hell? How could a new government come in and proceed to confiscate her books just like that? Irmgard Keun has a childlike propensity to question absolutely everything. Why is it that way? Where are my books? Is that just? Is it lawful? And if it isn't lawful, how can we change it right now? She has a sunny view of the world, even this

*The official writers' organization in Nazi Germany, in which membership was compulsory.

new one. But no one can keep looking at it that way. Not when reality keeps getting darker, and more dangerous—and more brown.

She boards the train at the beginning of May. The main thing is to get out of the land of the brown plague, of injustice, and of those who ban books. She wants to get to the sea. It widens her thoughts, she feels. She decides to go to Ostend, where she went on holidays with her parents. And she sets off. "Behind me, a country; in front of me, the whole world." She gets there on the fourth of May. She sees the promenade, the beach, the bistros, the casino, the whole free, informal world, and is enchanted.

Recently she has signed a contract with the publishing house of Allert de Lange. The editor Walter Landauer has obtained it for her. Right after she reaches Ostend, she receives 300 guilders as an advance on her new book, along with three articles, individually packed and delivered to her hotel room by way of a greeting from Landauer. The world of the émigrés has been waiting for her.

. . .

She travels to Brussels for a day. She's been told she could get to know Hermann Kesten there. She's read one novel of his thus far, *The Charlatan*. She meets him in the lobby of a large hotel. And he is the first man in this Belgian summer to be captivated by her magic. He sees her from a distance and thinks she looks like the kind of girl you would immediately want to go dancing with.

But that changes in a flash. Now what Hermann Kesten most wants is to talk with her, listen to her, and watch her as she talks: "We hadn't even sat down at a table with a cup of coffee and a glass of wine before she was speaking about Germany, with flashing eyes and her red, witty mouth. She talked about this exotic new Germania in a careful semiwhisper, with the boldest expressions and images. Her white silk blouse and her blond hair fluttered as if in the wildest wind, her eyes and her hands spoke volumes too, and she talked both from her heart and her head. She was naïve and brilliant, witty and despairing, folksy and fiery and no longer a girl you wanted to go dancing with, but a prophetess in accusatory mode, a chiding preacher, a political creature watching an entire civilization silt up. With every fiber she talked and laughed and mocked and mourned."

They talk for hours. Kesten soaks up her energy, her laugh, and her rage like a man dying of thirst. Kesten is thirty-six years old, left Germany immediately after the Nazis took power, and is the uncrowned king of émigré society. He needs the proximity of his friends, the poets, most of all. Later Stefan Zweig names him as the "protective father of all those who had been scattered across the world."

Kesten will write one of the most affectionate books about the world of the émigrés to appear after the war. It's called *My Friends the Poets*. He always writes in cafés, talks as he writes, and writes as he talks, indeed he needs conversation in order to be able to write at all.

He simply makes his home in the circles that gather of an evening in Nice, in Sanary-sur-Mer, in Paris, in Amsterdam, and here in Ostend. Moreover he has influence; he was formerly an editor at the publishing firm of Gustav Kiepenheuer and now, in tandem with Landauer, he runs the German department at Allert de Lange. He is a large force within the small market of German texts in exile. Somehow he seems to be everywhere, and Roth is right to call him a joker. Kesten is always concerned to be in a good mood, he has the deepest laugh lines in any face among the émigrés, but he suffers just as much from the isolation of exile as any of the others.

From Ostend he writes to his friend Franz Schoenberner: "It's a dreadful job, particularly since the prospects are so laughable. The first and last consolation is what we writers, more or less in self-mockery, have come to call the joy in our work."

He struggles to hold on to this joy. Which only increases

the importance of this recent meeting with the woman from Germany who knows one of his books, admires him, and is proud to meet him. She finds him incredibly clever and nice and witty. Though when he tells her what he's working on right now—Philip II, king of Spain, sixteenth century—she's downcast. Please! Why are they all writing works of history? On arrival, the publishing house has sent her a whole parcel of the latest émigré publications: Alfred Neumann's *The Empire*, Joseph Roth's *Hundred Days*, Bertolt Brecht's *Threepenny Opera*. When, if not now, will they get around to the present, will they *have* to get around to the present? Their books are banned in Germany anyhow. So there's no need to use history to hedge around what has to be written, most urgently, about the here and now.

But they lack immediate insight, direct contact with the Germany of today. What reaches them is only rumor or propaganda. All they know here is a travesty, or a yearning, or a nightmare. Barely amenable to being transmuted into good literature.

Which is why what Hermann Kesten in Brussels wants most of all to talk about is this: How is it in Germany today? How bad is it? How is the mood among sensible people? Is there any hope, any sign, that it's going to end sometime? Her talk is lively, original, and vivid. But what it tells him is fundamentally appalling and offers no hope of an early end. She describes "a Germany in which grocers and sergeants' widows were executing Nietzsche's philosophical ideas. A Germany with cheerless crude chants and threatening harangues on the radio, full of the prolonged artificial ecstasies of massed marches, Party rallies, Heil Hitlers, and festivals. A Germany filled with intoxicated petits bourgeois. Intoxicated because they had been given power." No, she has brought no hope from this country. But she brings energy and contrariness and, most of all, a delight in the world of the émigrés that its inhabitants, who have had to live in it for the last three years, have long since lost. Irmgard Keun is like a little girl who cannot believe she's now allowed to join this quasi-secret society. "I'm the only Aryan here!" she crows in a letter home. It's what she'd dreamed of in Germany. And now she's really here.

. . .

Okay, it's sometimes a bit lonely at the beginning, many of the émigrés haven't yet arrived, it's cold, misty, and windy. She often sits on one of the bistro terraces overlooking the promenade in defiance of the weather, with a white headscarf and a brightly colored coat. In front of her, a little heap of cooked shrimp, a teapot, a newspaper, and blank sheets of paper. She's totally absorbed in herself and writes. It's her novel about Germany, the one she's received an advance for. It's to be called *After Midnight*. She writes, "I stand on the street, the night is my home. Am I drunk? Am I mad? The voices and noises that surrounded me fell away like a coat; I'm freezing. The lights are going out. I'm alone."

Irmgard Keun has left behind a husband and also a lover. She's long ceased to love her husband, he understands not one word of her objections to these new times. Her lover, Arnold Strauss, is Jewish, a doctor, and left for America shortly after the Nazis took power. She does love him, a little at least, but hates the problem-free nature of his existence, hates it that he's instantly settling down in America and feeling at home, as if none of it's an adventure, or a challenge, or ominous. She writes him lots of letters, doesn't pretend to any longing she doesn't feel, but asks him regularly for money, gifts, and the necessities of life for a woman. Strauss is also married, lives in the United States with his wife, and loves Irmgard Keun more than anything in the world. He would rather give up his life in America today, not tomorrow, and get divorced in order to marry Irmgard Keun. But nothing could be further from her mind, now that she's just won this great freedom.

"I love you, but the idea of marrying you is a dirty one," she writes from Ostend at the beginning of June to Montgomery, West Virginia, where he's living and working. "I would rather let myself be beaten to death in a German concentration camp than live the rest of my life gratefully and humbly by your side."

Clearly. But it doesn't diminish his love in any way—on the contrary—nor his readiness to send money to the woman he adores. Irmgard Keun is delighted, keeps thinking up new demands, and writes her book.

■ ■ ■

For more than a month she's been living in the Hôtel de la Couronne in the center of Ostend, right next to the station, with a view onto the harbor. It's June now, and summer is slowly arriving. The first bathing guests are coming in, the promenade is coming to life, there are parasols, and men in swimming trunks, and the bathing huts are being pushed into position along the beach.

Irmgard Keun goes to visit the Kisches* for a few days. It's not far from Ostend to Bredene. A tram goes around the harbor basin and then as far as the big sand dune, and the whole journey takes twenty minutes. At the other end, the Kisches are ensconced in a hotel where they've already been living for several weeks. Irmgard Keun loves

* Egon Erwin Kisch was the most famous German reporter of the day.

the company of the Kisches, and they love her. All this new life that has come whirling in from Germany this spring to their little congregation of émigrés!

She shows the first thirty pages of her new book to Egon Erwin Kisch. And Kisch is wildly enthusiastic, so enthusiastic that he vanishes upstairs to his room, leaving Irmgard Keun downstairs with his wife. It's half an hour before he comes down again. He's written letters, one to Landauer to congratulate him on this fantastic author, one to his American publisher to recommend this sensational German writer and her new book, and one to friends in Paris, to ask them to invite Irmgard Keun to come and lecture on the current situation in Germany. Keun is enthused by his enthusiasm but also by his revolutionary élan, his fighting Communist spirit, his optimism, his undauntedness, and his certainty about the victory to come. "You don't know anyone like this," she immediately writes to Arnold Strauss in America, "and this desperate labor to create a new, democratic Germany!" It is glorious.

Kisch tells her about his epic journey to Australia two years ago as a delegate to the Anti-War Congress in October 1934. The Australian government did not let him land—he supposedly was a danger to the country's safety. Whereupon a group of forty sympathizers who'd already made it to shore hired a motorboat and circled Kisch's enormous steamer. He jumped down into the little boat from a height of eighteen feet, to be greeted by an anti-war banner they had hoisted. Kisch broke a leg but was finally allowed ashore and hailed by jubilant crowds; the entire world press reported the story. And in Australia, the story went, the movement against war and Fascism, which previously hadn't amounted to more than a small group, became a mass phenomenon. Egon Erwin Kisch was its hero for several weeks.

Slightly less heroic is the fact that he's been working on his book about the trip for eighteen months now and still can't finish it. He already spent the summer here last year to do just that, but he's still sitting on it. It's supposed to be called *Landing in Australia*, and he laughs uneasily when he mentions it. But he laughs. Egon Erwin Kisch likes to laugh at himself. He chain-smokes, always has some Communists visiting, and is always hatching plans with them. Irmgard Keun is smitten. She calls him Egonek, as do all his friends.

She spends a few wonderful days with him and his wife passing the time lying in the dune with Gisela, swimming, doing exercises, and writing to Montgomery. "I've gone completely native and look like a Negress wearing a yellow wig."

Then one day Egonek says to her: We're going to Ostend together today. To the Café Flore. There's someone I have to introduce you to.

They go over by train. The promenade is pullulating with vacationers—children in bright hats, sun, the easy life. They sit down in the Flore in the shade under the awning, with a view of the beach, and are ordering aperitifs when two men arrive. The one is in a pale suit, with waistcoat and tie, well-trimmed mustache and thick hair, and dark darting eyes; self-confident, worldly, with a firm stride, like an elegant shrew in his Sunday best. And right behind him, a smaller man, a trifle hunched, in a dark suit, narrow officer's trousers, a little potbelly protruding above them, a striped bowtie, a tuft of hair coming down over his forehead, a pale unkempt mustache over his upper lip, and a slightly wavering gait. He looks like a mournful seal that has wandered accidentally onto dry land. Egon Erwin Kisch and Gisela greet the man in the pale suit with friendly laughter and introduce Irmgard Keun. It's Stefan Zweig, and shyly she gives him her hand. Meantime Kisch has run to the swaying seal and is slapping him on the back with full force. "What? No crown? No ermine? What's wrong, you old Hapsburg Jew?" is his joyous form of greeting. "Very funny, you old Bolshevik Jew," accompanied by a rumbling laugh, is the response. And Kisch, cigarette in corner of mouth, kicks off a euphoric round of conversation, interrupting Zweig and Keun in their first slightly stiff exchanges to speed along the process of these other two getting to know each other as well. They shake hands in friendly fashion. Irmgard Keun sees his delicate white hands protruding from the black sleeves, she sees the wispy blond mustache and the ash on his jacket. "My skin said 'yes' immediately," she writes later. She looks at him, looks at his blue eyes, sees the bad teeth that he tries hard to keep hidden under the long mustache, sees his sadness. "When I first saw Joseph Roth back then in Ostend, I had the feeling I was seeing someone who would die of sheer sadness in a matter of hours. His round, blue eyes stared almost blindly in despair and his voice seemed to founder under a burden of grief. This impression was later blurred by the fact that Roth was not only sad back then, he was also the most accomplished and vigorous hater."

The two of them are lost to the rest of the little group that evening. Roth wordlessly pulls her down onto a chair by his side. He's mistrustful. She's not Jewish, he doesn't know her, he doesn't know any of her books. Why is she here? Because of her repugnance at the country, the people, and those in power, she says. Aha. And why has she come just now? She talks about her husband, her mother, and her Jewish lover in America. Roth is still mistrustful. Not because he thinks she's an informer. He simply doesn't accept that she's only now taken the decision to come. Emigration brooks no hesitation and no ambivalence and no delay. But naturally she also impresses him too. Because, as a non-Jew, she willingly gave up everything, and because she's fighting the German authorities in complete outrage. The longer she talks, the more quietly and greedily he listens. About Germany, about life there, about Berlin. He hasn't been there for three and a half years. He wants to know everything.

And she loves his curiosity, his acute attention, his wide stare, his follow-up questions, his quick judgments, as wicked as they are surprising and spot on. She knows his books *Job* and *Radetsky March*, she thinks very highly of them and is astonished that he is as good a storyteller, if not better, in conversation than in his books. No one knows what in his stories is made up and what is actual experience. He just loves to tell stories, and in particular he's loving telling them to sunburned Irmgard Keun, brought here by old Kisch. Later she will say she has never met, either before or since, a man with the sexual magnetism of Joseph Roth that evening in the Café Flore. What she really wants is to go off with him immediately, no matter where. Just to keep listening and talking. To be with him. And drink.

That too is a bond between them from the very beginning. They realize immediately that they are both seasoned drinkers, artists of drink, skilled in its basics, understanding why drink is essential both to life and to writing. "You only have to open a newspaper, and you know how idiotic it is to be persisting in writing at all," Irmgard Keun explains in a letter to Arnold Strauss concerning her drinking. "If you want to write, you have to suppress your thoughts and your awareness of the flood to come, and of war etc. Otherwise you can't write at all. And that's why you need alcohol. The only thing that matters is to drink well and wisely. The artist's calling is irretrievably, inescapably bound to your moods."

Finally someone who understands me, thinks Roth and thinks Keun. Someone you can drink with uninhibitedly, who knows it's the only way to endure, that abstinence may perhaps in the long run prolong life, but in the short run the here and now makes it quite impossible. In addition, here in Ostend, Roth is constantly accompanied by his conscience, Stefan Zweig, who is doing everything in his power to stop Roth from drinking. When he joins him in the bistro, Roth drinks milk, to spare himself the reproaches and to use this exaggerated obedience to make fun of Zweig. Zweig is like a mother to him. He sees that it's going to kill Roth, that it's destroying his writing, no matter how much Roth tells himself that it's drink that makes his art possible at all. "I cannot discipline my writing without dissipating myself physically," he once wrote to Zweig. Roth is an advanced alcoholic. His legs and feet are badly swollen, to the point where it's almost impossible for him to put on a pair of shoes. For years now, he's had to throw up every morning, sometimes for hours. He eats almost nothing. Going out to eat in a restaurant strikes him as an eccentric waste of money, that only a rich man like Stefan Zweig could dream up. Nevertheless, Zweig tries to convince him to eat a meal day after day. This summer in Ostend it even frequently works.

...

EGON ERWIN KISCH IS CONSTANTLY surrounded by his Communist fellow fighters. They discuss the political situation like commanders, discuss new strategies in the battle against European Fascism, plan congresses, committees, and calls to arms. Willi Muenzenberg is the charismatic leader of their circle. During the Weimar Republic he was the Communist press czar of Germany; he had set up an entire empire of daily newspapers, weekly newspapers, and illustrated magazines, with circulation in the millions. He owned newspapers all around the world, nineteen dailies in Japan alone, and a film production company in Russia. Willi Muenzenberg was the embodiment of the public face of Communism. Now, after the banning of all his German publications and many of those in other countries around the globe, he is the powerful chief of the agitprop department of the Comintern. He's no intellectual, anything but. He's a bear, he's built like a cupboard, indeed in his youth he worked as a carpenter. He's a worker, he comes from a working-class family, and he speaks with a broad Thuringian accent. He doesn't take part in struggles over the Party line or in intrigues. He's a pragmatist, a propagandist. When he enters, silence falls over archdukes, bankers, and Socialist ministers. When he slips into a room, it's as if he were breaking through a wall. And his co-workers anxiously search his face for signs of his mood that day. He's a charismatic leader of men, always surrounded by his closest co-workers, the three musketeers. These are his secretary, Hans Schultz; Emil the chauffeur; and Yupp, his bodyguard. You never meet him without the other three.

Willi Muenzenberg has ideas that come spouting out of him all day long. Hans Schultz is usually kept busy until far into the night writing down these ideas, assigning tasks, composing calls to action. Schultz is a tall, lame, discreet, timid man. Muenzenberg delivers the headlines, Schultz must execute them. Arthur Koestler once described how such a task got formulated: "Write to Feuchtwanger. Tell him to get articles and so on. Tell him we need a pamphlet from him; we'll smuggle ten thousand of them into Germany; about the saving of our cultural heritage etc., leave the rest to him, hugs and kisses. Then buy a book on meteorology, Hans, study the highs and lows and so on, find out how the wind blows across the Rhine, how many leaflets, small format, we can attach to a balloon, where in Germany the balloons are likely to land, and so on. Then, Hans, get in touch with a couple of balloon manufacturers, tell them it's for export to Venezuela, ask cost estimates for ten thousand balloons. Then, Hans . . ." And Hans whirls. There's no proposal he doesn't follow up on. All this is backed up by Willi's cat's-paw, as they call him: Otto Katz, a.k.a. André Simone, as he styles himself here in exile. Muenzenberg's adjutant, ambassador of the invisible Willi, his face to the world, and above all his voice. He speaks multiple languages, Muenzenberg speaks only Thuringian; he's an excellent journalist, Muenzenberg not at all. When it's a matter of rounding up donations in Muenzenberg's name from sympathizers all around the world, Otto Katz is the man. He executes Muenzenberg's propaganda strategy: Whoever gives money for something feels he belongs to it and has an inner connection. The more money someone gives, the stronger the connection. Muenzenberg's connections thus extend far into the liberal bourgeoisie.

Katz is the ideal man to be out in the world working for his chief and for the movement. Charming, clever, and witty, with a soft face, a bit sly, always full of sparkling talk. When he smokes, he closes his left eye. Over time it becomes a quirk, and soon he's closing it to think, even when there's no cigarette. He comes from Prague, was the director of Erwin Piscator's theater on the Nollendorfplatz in Berlin, accumulated a mound of debts, went totally bankrupt, and wanted to commit suicide in despair, when he met Muenzenberg, who installed him at one of his newspapers. "I fished him out of the Landwehr canal," Muenzenberg likes to say when anyone asks him how he met Katz.

Another member of the circle is the journalist Arthur Koestler, born in Budapest in 1905. He has received money from Muenzenberg to come to Bredene, near Ostend, and write a sequel to *The Good Soldier Schweik*. And he writes and argues and observes Muenzenberg and his collaborators. He sees their petty jealousies; he also suspects that Otto Katz is reporting on his chief to Moscow. Muenzenberg is not liked by the Party ideologues, by the Germans Ulbricht* and Pieck,† by the ultraorthodox or the loyalists to the Party line. They're all working to bring him down. Moscow Central views his independence with the deepest mistrust. Muenzenberg senses that his downfall is coming; he also senses that Katz is informing on him, but he needs him. And he certainly does not conceal from his adjutant how much he despises him.

Arthur Koestler will write about all this later on. He is already, even now, too independent for the Party and perhaps also too Jewish. An early convert to Zionism, he moved to the Holy Land, full of enthusiasm, but was soon obliged to sustain himself by selling lemonade in

---

*First head of state of the GDR after the war.
† First president of the GDR after the war.

Haifa; rather sobered, he moved back to Berlin, became a reporter for the Ullstein* paper *Berliner Zeitung am Mittag*, and traveled through the Soviet Union and the Near East; he also flew over Antarctica in an airship. His first big success in book form had taken place two years before, in 1934, with the first volume of his *Encyclopedia of Sexual Knowledge*. But now, in exile, he is nonetheless dependent on the Party's goodwill and its money.

When Roth joins the group, he behaves as if he's oblivious to the Communists at Kisch's table. Even when they make fun of the monarchists, it's as if he doesn't hear them. Roth has eyes and ears only for Kisch, whom he loves for his humor, his warmheartedness, and his honesty. Joseph Roth does not permit himself to be mocked by many people for his emperor worship. But if it's Kisch, gladly. Even if he had wanted to be spared the jokers this summer, Kisch makes himself easy to love. "Now, Sepp"—he actually calls Joseph Roth Sepp; he's the only person allowed to do that—"what's your emperor doing in Steenokkerzeel? Does he wear his crown to breakfast?" he asks after the exiled heir to the throne. And Roth amiably, dignifiedly, calmly, replies, "Yes, an invisible crown."

*The Ullsteins were major newspaper proprietors and publishers in Berlin.

...

Then on July 13 the newspapers report the murder of the monarchist leader of the opposition, José Calvo Sotelo, in Spain, the first officers' revolt, and on July 17, under the leadership of the Fascist general Francisco Franco, rebellion against the democratically elected government of the Popular Front breaks out in Spain. From then on, Kisch's table becomes an overcrowded Communist resistance–cum–information bureau. As is clear to them all, the Spanish Civil War is going to be a laboratory for the coming war in Europe, a battle of ideologies between the great powers of the Continent. How will Nazi Germany react? And Mussolini's Italy? And the Soviet Union? What does it mean for the newly elected Popular Front government in France?

And above all, how can those nonfascistic European countries be mobilized to reach in on the side of the Spanish government? Arthur Koestler is the first who is determined to get to Spain. Immediately, Muenzenberg calms him down. "What do you want there? In the trenches. What good will that do us?" Besides which there's something he has to tell him—the Party isn't interested in any new *Schweik* book. He can stop writing. Koestler doesn't care. He wants to get to Spain. He still has his press pass from the Hungarian newspaper *Pester Lloyd*—maybe that'll get him into the country. Muenzenberg's eyes suddenly light up. That sounds really good. Hungary is after all a semi-fascistic country. It's really, really good. And he has a much better idea for him than the trenches.

"Go to Franco's HQ and take a little look around," he says with a contented smile. The goal: to find evidence of German and Italian intervention on the side of Franco. And Koestler gets going.

Joseph Roth is only marginally interested in all this. The electric atmosphere of their readiness to fight is foreign to him. But his Austria in these weeks is also in a worse situation than ever. His fatherland signed an agreement with Nazi Germany on July 11. Or is this somehow good news? Is it a cunning chess move by the Schuschnigg regime to protect itself in the long term from the growing influence of Germany? Joseph Roth has no illusions. It's a further step on the road to the annexation of Austria to Nazi Germany, a further step toward catastrophe. The agreement provides for an amnesty for imprisoned members of the Nazi Party, which is banned in Austria, and the lifting of the ban against several German newspapers; the Schuschnigg government also commits itself to bringing two National Socialists, one as a minister and the other as secretary of state, into the administration. The Austrian chancellor thereby hopes to preserve Austrian sovereignty going forward. But he's only opening the door a little wider for the Germans. He's neither the first nor the last politician to think that Adolf Hitler can be placated permanently with concessions. It's a sign of weakness. And nobody sees this so exactly and so worriedly as the two Austrians at the seaside in Belgium. One of them, the one wearing narrow officer's trousers, in particular.

．．．

HE MOVED IN WITH HER at once, only days after they first set eyes on each other in the Café Flore. He lives with her in the Hôtel de la Couronne with its view of the sailboats and the station. The others can't believe it. This young, suntanned, merry woman and the alcoholic Roth? How can it be? And where will it lead? "She's trying to wean him off drinking, and he's trying to wean her onto it. I think he's winning," says Kisch. Stefan Zweig is not convinced, but he's happy at first, because he sees how it's giving new life to his old friend, putting him back on his feet again and helping him to get over the parting from Manga Bell. But then he also reverts to being the concerned brother who sees that Roth, when he's sitting with Keun, is heavily increasing his intake of schnapps. The ban on it, which was supposed to obtain in Belgium, is easily evaded by practiced drinkers like Keun and Roth.

Keun describes it thus: "Unfortunately the drinks in Belgium are mostly pure shit. No wonder you get poisoned in a country where schnapps is banned. I ask you, what are you supposed to drink? The beer here is shit. Wine is a possibility only if it is really expensive. The sweet aperitifs turn your stomach after the fourth glass, plus they give you a headache. Naturally I have bars where I get schnapps. It's always insanely expensive and almost never any good. You should earn enough as a writer to be able to drink one to two bottles of *decent* dry Champagne per day once you're within eight or nine weeks of finishing a novel. It's a shitty time, and this would put you in the right mood to work, and you wouldn't get ill."

When Irmgard Keun sends this letter to her lover in America, she's already been with Joseph Roth, the king of grumps, the king of curses, and the king of all hates, for a month. Most of what they've done during these weeks is to laugh, so often and so loud that they're in tears. Their favorite occupation is to make fun of Stefan Zweig and his good nature, his naïve, unshakable belief in the good in people, his love of humanity. "It can't be genuine," Roth keeps saying, although he of all people knows better.

Zweig takes him to a good tailor to have a new pair of trousers made for his suit. The tailor refuses to follow the narrow officer's cut demanded by Roth, but Roth is delighted with the result nonetheless. But when he is sitting next day on the market square with Irmgard Keun and Hermann Kesten at a bistro table that looks like a beer mug, he orders three glasses of liqueur and empties them over his jacket one after the other, to the wild applause of his girlfriend, as Hermann Kesten recalls later. "What are you doing?" asks Kesten. "I'm punishing Stefan Zweig," Roth replies. "That's how millionaires are! They take us to the tailor, but they forget to buy us a jacket to go with the trousers!" Three days later Stefan Zweig indeed orders a jacket to be made for him too. "He's a genius," Zweig says to Kesten. "A genius like Verlaine, a genius like Villon!" And Roth is proud of his new jacket, and proud of the fact that he hasn't behaved humbly with Zweig.

Kesten is the object of mirth too. Over his terrible books, and over his large stomach and his belief that if he just keeps sucking it in under the bistro table, nobody will notice it. "Diamond Hermann" is what Roth calls him when Kesten isn't there, because he once had a jewelry business with his sister. At least Roth persists in saying so, even though nobody else has ever heard a word about it. The only nonliterary place Hermann Kesten has ever worked in was his mother's junk shop.

Kesten wrote a story about Ostend two years ago that was published in Klaus Mann's exile periodical *The Collection*. A horror story set in the midst of a Belgian summer idyll: "As the first star emitted its timid pinpoint of light against the end of the sky in a faintly green glow and a smokestack on the horizon announced the approach of the steamer from England, the bather and the jeweler dug the dead woman out of the sand. She was already decomposing, but the sand-damaged clothes were still new and pretty. The corpse's body was slim and well built; only the face was horrifying, iridescent green and blue, in the colors of the ocean. But the gaping jaws were filled with brightly glittering sand, like a suffocated scream encased in stone."

Hermann Kesten tells the story of the murder of this woman, the teacher Adrienne, daughter of a pious Ostend tailor, in a manner that is both meticulous and chilling. "Her death may have been grisly, fodder for newspapers, but her life was worse." He tells of her great disappointed love, her rape in the dunes of Bredene, the way she is buried defenseless in the sand, and how two innocent people are declared guilty and put to death, and how a young boy, Paul, could have prevented this but remains silent. How the real perpetrator and two accomplices are also found guilty and hanged. Kesten writes about the lights on the fishing boats that sail out in the early hours of the morning into the dark and the open sea; he writes about the dance bar Mexiko, the boisterous atmosphere, the colorful Chinese lanterns in July, the cries of the seagulls, and the boy who wants only to stay silent and watch what happens. He ends thus: "It only remains to report that the boy Paul, whose strange frame of mind cost two good men their lives, is now fifteen and is already writing beautiful verses that promise a delightful poetic talent.

"The boy's appetite is good. His sleep is undisturbed.

His schoolmates give no cause for concern. In the warm summer nights, particularly when there's a full moon, lovers like to lie at the foot of the dune where they found beautiful Adrienne, choked to death, her open mouth full of sand like a scream in human form."

The beach of Ostend, the dunes of Bredene, writers who do not write about murder, lovers in the sand, and a strangled cry. Kesten has erected a literary monument to the terrible aspects of this town of émigrés. And every summer the writers return.

. . .

Finally the Tollers arrive too, from London, on the direct ship from Dover. Wherever they surface, they're stars, with a nimbus of beauty and fame. The Socialist and his goddess, as people call them. The actress Christiane Grautoff is radiantly lovely and unbelievably young. A few days ago she was still on stage in London as Rachel in Ernst Toller's play *No More Peace*, translated by W. H. Auden. She received good reviews and was loving her life as an actress in London. Toller is talked about all over Europe as a playwright and champion of revolution. He was the celebrated playwright of the Weimar Republic and the tribune of the Munich Soviet Republic, whose leadership of the revolution cost him five years in jail. He didn't allow it to break him, either in the sweep of his writing or in his fighting revolutionary stance. In London he gave a speech as president of the International Association of Writers for the Defence of Culture at the opening of their congress, with the call: "No, no one can flee the present fight, particularly in a time when Fascism has raised the doctrine of the totalitarian state to the level of law. The dictator demands of the writer that he become the obedient mouthpiece of the ruling worldview. There is one good aspect to this claim of the dictators: it makes us reflect, it teaches us anew to treasure the spiritual values that we have come to undervalue because they were so often misused." It is also his personal experience that he is pointing to in political terms when he cries, "Only he who has lost his freedom learns to love it truly." And he closes with the acknowledgment that pulls together the lessons of his life and his life's mission: "We do not love politics for politics' sake. We take part in political life today, but we believe it is not the least significant aspect of our battle to free future mankind from the wretched competition of interests that goes by the name of 'politics' today. We know the limits of what we can achieve. We are plowmen, and we don't know if we will be reapers. But we've learned that 'fate' is an excuse. *We* make fate! We want to be true, we want to be courageous, and we want to be human."

Many battle-weary émigrés take new heart from Ernst

Toller. From his clear-headedness, his bright face, his refusal to give up, his repeated appeals to the fighting spirit and to the optimism of those who are now landless. And his speeches of encouragement are all the more convincing because they are addressed first and foremost to himself. Ernst Toller is subject to severe depressions, is weary of life, and pessimistic to the point of self-abnegation. His lover and now for twelve months his wife, Christiane, will tell of this later and of how she always had to pack a length of rope in the top layer of his suitcase, so that he would have a final way to escape.

To the outside world, the lives of the couple are among the most glittering of the émigré community. That spring they raced along the Côte d'Azur in a sports car from town to town, never staying put in any one place. Ernst Toller has long, recurrent phases in which he is unable to write, not so much as a word, in which he is tormented by the blank page and flees the void in his car. "Then we went speedily down the coast and back. To Monte Carlo, where I won five hundred francs in the Casino and thought I'd broken the bank. Who did we see in Nice? I have no idea any more. E.T. raced around in misery, and I with him."

When Ernst Toller met Christiane in the summer of 1932, she was fifteen years old and already a star. They called her the Wunderkind. She had already acted on stage with Fritz Kortner, made a film with Henny Porten, and was the celebrated star this season in Max Reinhardt's legendary production of *A Midsummer's Night Dream* and in Kästner's *Emil and the Detectives*. The critic Alfred Kerr wrote of her, "Child, when you come to understand what you're saying—" But perhaps she already understood a great deal. In any case she regularly visited the apartment of the almost-forty-year-old playwright Ernst Toller, who shared it with his friend Fritz Landshoff, the publisher of Kiepenheuer. Toller asked him in some embarrassment if he was going to be home in the afternoon, as he was expecting a visitor. The latter reassured him that no, he was going to be in the publishing house. And as Landshoff was going down the stairs later, he met "a very young, very blond, very adorable girl" coming up, who seemed familiar to him. That evening Toller told him he'd had a visit from Christiane Grautoff. She wrote later that "E.T. and I had a very unusual relationship. It was wholly platonic. First of all I really was still a minor, and secondly E.T. was afraid of virgins. We had long conversations about his life and my life, his thoughts and my thoughts. I swam around in his poems as if I were in a pond whose waters were totally opaque, and there were water lilies on the surface and from time to time I picked them."

In 1933 she was supposed to appear in the Nazi propaganda film *Hans Westmar*, but she declined and accompanied Ernst Toller into exile. As soon as she turned eighteen, in April 1935, they married in London.

Wherever she goes with him, writers almost go crazy at the sight of her youth and her beauty. The German writer Arnold Zweig is even supposed to have climbed through her window in Nice one night. "It must have been really hard for the poor thing, because first of all he was too fat and second of all he was too blind to climb in or out of anywhere," she says later. She doesn't think much of the émigrés' evening palavers: "They would argue, and sometimes the writers read out their poems or pieces. I knitted all my opinions into beautiful angora pullovers for E.T. I had a lot to say, mainly that they were all too old and too boring and they kept saying the same things and most certainly they would never be right. But they often were, so then I knitted a bit quicker and made mistakes in the stitches."

But she's happy to be here at the beach with Gisela Kisch and Irmgard Keun, passionate swimmers all three. And on good days Ernst Toller goes swimming with them, athletically proud, and he swims far out, farther and farther, until Christiane fears for his life.

At all other times he barely lets her out of his sight and

is unbelievably jealous. Besides which he worries about her fragility, her heedlessness, her absolute belief in people's goodness. For example, he forbids her to talk to Erika Mann. She's depraved, he says. She's allowed, on the other hand, to talk to Klaus Mann—she's even a friend of his. But the Mann children are not in Ostend this summer; a few days ago they drove through Spain in their sports car with their friends Annemarie Schwarzenbach and Fritz Landshoff and lay on the same beach in Majorca where bombs will fall later in the summer. Otherwise the two Manns are always present wherever more than three émigrés meet on a beach, only to disappear again as quickly as they arrived.

The second person Toller has explicitly warned his wife against is, however, here, but the worried playwright deems the situation to be unthreatening. Later Christiane writes, "I was allowed to meet Joseph Roth, although he was a sadist; because he already had his victim, a ravishingly beautiful woman, E.T. saw no danger for me. He shielded me and taught me to see what was behind people's façades."

Joseph Roth—a sadist? Egon Erwin Kisch once puts it this way over the course of the summer with a laugh: "Sepp always expects a certain submissiveness in women." But he picked the wrong one in Irmgard Keun. "We're driving through the night, all the lights swaying along with us. My head is lying in Franz's lap. I must make myself seem weaker than I am, so that he can feel strong and able to love me." She wrote that in Ostend, in her novel *After Midnight*. She is a strong young woman and cunning. And the passage in her novel fits most of the women who belong to the ever-growing group this summer in Belgium. Showing oneself to be weaker than one is, so that the men can feel stronger, is also true of quiet Lotte Altmann, Gisela Kisch, and Christiane Grautoff, of course, with her clever knitting; even Willi Muenzenberg's wife, Babette, from a high-bourgeois family in Potsdam, beautiful and cool and patrician and speaking High German without a trace of a dialect, often observes her Thuringian bear with an ironic eye but would never dream of contradicting one of his rapid, vehement theories and calls to action.

•••

ONCE AGAIN THEY'RE ALL SITTING in the Flore, this company
in free fall, trying one more time this summer to feel like
a group of vacationers. Trying to pretend that they're carefree. Really, it's just a great long trip they've been on for
years. Far from home, traveling with friends, in Paris, Nice,
Sanary-sur-Mer, Amsterdam, Marseille, Ostend. And at
some point there'll be a return journey. But when? The
more urgent this question becomes, the less often it is
posed. With every day of this vacation that goes by, any
return becomes less plausible. They all know it. But it's
never discussed. Optimism is a duty. There's a length of
rope in the suitcase, but nobody talks about it.

Today once again they're all trying not to turn immediately to politics and pore over the ominous news of the
day. But it's hopeless. There simply isn't anything to talk
about that is not political.

Egon Erwin Kisch tries it with sports. Which these days
means Max Schmeling. Kisch has known and admired him
for a long time. They were neighbors at the Scharmuet-
zelsee near Berlin, Kisch has attended many of his fights,
and from a distance he has recently watched Schmeling

refuse to bow to Nazi pressure to separate from his Czech wife and his Jewish manager, Joe Jacobs. And Kisch has of course read everything about the fight in New York on June 19 and has been getting on everyone's nerves for days with his vocal admiration. The way Schmeling decked the "Brown Bomber," Joe Louis. And most of all, the way he impressed America even before the fight began with his bold, cool remark about a weakness of his opponent's: "I have seen something." That's the classic Schmeling under-statement that Kisch loves so much. "Ha! 'I have seen something'! As if I'd prepped him in advance!" cries Kisch. "Modesty, self-possession, and mystery, all in one sentence! Max is one of us." And he explains to the table all over again just what Max saw: that after attacking, Joe Louis lets his left hand drop a little, and that this brief hole pro-vides the critical opening for a counterattack. After twelve rounds the supposedly unbreakable Joe Louis went down, and Kisch loves to imitate the decisive punch, the way he thinks it must have been. "And now he's an advertise-ment in America for the criminal Olympics," Kersten yells back, while Kisch is still in full flood. Which brings them back to the usual theme. The leading news out of Berlin these days is the preparation for the Olympic Games. The whole world will be coming to the German capital. The regime has been busy donning a disguise for weeks, divest-ing itself of the visible signs of anti-Jewish and anti-foreign policies and presenting itself as a civil state committed to international friendship. All "Forbidden to Jews" signs have been taken down. "And have you heard?" asks Toller. "*Der Stürmer* has been censored for weeks. Not to remove any statements, just the anti-Semitic passages." "Wonderful! So now they're selling blank paper!" is Roth's bitterly mocking retort.

In truth, this is the nub of their anxiety: that the world will allow itself to be deceived this summer in Berlin. That Goebbels will succeed in convincing the world of the Nazis' peaceable intentions and putting it to sleep, confirming its belief that Germany is harmless. England has just announced it intends to shrink its navy. The League of Nations has lifted the sanctions against Italy that had been imposed in the wake of the conflict in Abyssinia. Mussolini's Italy celebrated, and Germany celebrated along with it.

The world will sleep, in order to live in peace. And the little group in Ostend hates its own powerlessness to the point of despair.

They prefer not to talk about the news that reached them from Geneva at the beginning of the month. The Czech journalist Stefan Lux, who is Jewish, committed suicide during the General Assembly of the League of Nations. In front of the packed plenum, to protest the league's and the world's inaction vis-à-vis the crimes being committed in Germany. The reaction was brief horror, a certain distaste for such fanaticism, some shoulder shrugging, and then things went on. Disarmament, negotiations, preparation for the Olympic Games in Berlin. It is appalling. Even suicide as a signal leaves this world indifferent. No, the name of Stefan Lux will preferably not be mentioned this summer.

Things are rather different as regards Etkar André. The Communists in particular, and Kisch most particularly, have been closely following the reporting on his trial. André is a Communist, born in Aachen in 1894; then, after his father's early death, he was raised in an orphanage in Belgium. In the Weimar Republic he was a member of Ernst Thaelmann's* closest circle and a much-loved leader of the workers in Hamburg. After the Reichstag fire he was arrested, just like Kisch. But unlike Kisch, he remained under arrest and still is. The charge: high treason and attempted murder of an SA man in Hamburg. The proof is laughably thin. Moreover, numerous foreign journalists are already in the country in advance of the Olympics, and they are following the trial attentively and reporting on it extensively. No one here in Ostend had expected his conviction. The death sentence shocks them all.

The moment when they hear word of the sentence is one of those situations when all cynicism and all internal

---

*Head of the German Communist Party.

rivalries are stilled. As they were after the death of Stefan Lux. It is in moments like these that the émigrés are fully aware of their powerlessness and the all-powerfulness of their enemies. White-faced hatred and fear and the hope for eventual revenge are the predominant emotions of the refugees. They have all read Etkar André's final words to the court. The pathos, the pride, the self-assuredness of a believer who knows himself to be innocent. "Your honor is not my honor, for we are divided by our worldviews, divided by class, divided by an abyss. If you are going to make the impossible possible here and send an innocent man to the block, then I am ready to walk that hard road. I want no mercy! I have lived as a fighter, and I will die as a fighter, and my last words will be: 'Long live Communism!'"

What is there to say? None of them doubts that the sentence will be carried out. Just as none of them doubts, deep down, that everything is going to end badly. The only thing is not to show despondency. Defeatism is a crime here at the shore.

It's better to bitch around together. The later the evening, the greater the sniping, the laughter, and the mockery. Of Klaus Mann, for example. Nice that he's not here for once. That announcement of his new novel in the *Pariser Tageszeitung*! Kesten is beside himself with laughter: the editors had announced the prepublication excerpt of *Mephisto* in the issue of June 20. The entire exile community had already known that Mann was writing a novel in which he was portraying his former brother-in-law Gustav Gruendgens in barely veiled terms as the prototypical opportunist of the present day. But the book's announcement by the *Tageszeitung* under the heading "Roman à Clef," with the name Gustav Gruendgens helpfully supplied as the key in question, was a real embarrassment. And that Klaus Mann, urged on by his friend and publisher Fritz Landshoff, then inflated the embarrassment to enormous proportions by sending a telegram flatly denying this, is the trigger for their universal derision and scorn. "My novel is not a roman à clef. The hero of the novel is a fictional character without any connection to specific persons. Klaus Mann." First to write such an obvious novel of revenge, then to promote it so provocatively before publication, and then helplessly to deny it all—it's a combination of naïveté and audacity that's too much for the seasoned writers around the table here in the Flore. Although they all like the driven, sensitive, handsome son of Thomas Mann. But he writes his books a little too fast, and he's too quick to fall into enthusiasms. A hothead, a fighter, and they can't help making fun of the emotionalism in his books, most particularly *Mephisto*, which is still being excerpted in the exile newspaper in Paris. Only Stefan Zweig admonishes the mocking Kesten in midflow to just say it to him in person instead.

He won't. And Zweig knows why. The reason Kesten is making sport of his friend's ineptitude is first and foremost that what Klaus Mann has written is effectively his, Kesten's, book. All of it—the idea, the story, the characters— were suggested to Klaus Mann by Kesten as material for a book more than six months ago. And the former wrote it at top speed, far too fast yet again, in Kesten's half-mistrustful, half-envious opinion. He can't come to grips with how quickly Mann has thrown the whole thing down onto paper. And now, in his cockiness, his indifference, and his well-intentioned naïveté, he's calling the success of the whole thing into question.

On November 15, 1935, Kesten had written the following to Klaus Mann in Amsterdam: "Because Landshoff told me you were looking for fresh material for your new novel, and because I myself am looking around for something for my own, I came up with this and that, and then something I think I would do very badly and you would do very well. In brief, I think you should write the story of a homosexual careerist in the Third Reich, and what I had in front of me was the figure you've already been toying with artistically (or so they tell me) in your mind, the Intendant of the State Theater, Gruendgens. (Title: *The Intendant*.)

I'm not thinking you should write a high political satire, but—almost—an apolitical novel, the model being Maupassant's 'Bel Ami,' which already inspired your uncle to discover the wonderful 'land of Cockaigne.' So no Hitler and Goering and Goebbels as characters, no agitprop, no Communist subversives, no Muenzenberg flourishes, but in some fashion the assassination of this Berlin actor whose name seems to be escaping me just at the moment. The whole thing in the ironic mirror of a hidden but easily detectable passion . . . To sum up: the Capital tells the story of how one becomes the Intendant.

"I think some story of this sort would work very well in your hands and with its description of the world of the Third Reich would offer great opportunities. I spoke with Landshoff about it, and he agreed with me."

Now, after Zweig has called him to account, Kesten tells the whole circle where Klaus Mann got the subject matter and the idea for this book. And when.

This in turn prompts Roth to tell his collected friends how, at Kesten's instigation, he reviewed his first novel for the *Frankfurter Zeitung*. Roth read it, didn't think it was very good, and fundamentally incomprehensible. That's what he wrote, and before publication he gave the piece to Kesten to read. The last two sentences ran: "I don't understand the novel. Perhaps Kesten is a great comedian." Kesten cut the penultimate sentence and excised the word *perhaps* from the last. Much better that way, he said to Roth, who allowed the text to appear in Kesten's version.

"Where would you be today without this text, Hermann?" Roth exclaims to the circle at large, and laughs. They all laugh too. They know that almost no other writer has as good connections to reviewers in the Weimar Republic and almost no one works them as intensively as Kesten. And they know that Joseph Roth actually reads very little but reviews a great deal. He doesn't need to read, he tells stories around the books and adds what he feels to be a somehow appropriate judgment. He likes writing about his own books too. And when he's in a particularly good mood, he pans them.

Right now he's actually reading something again. Not to write about it, but because it's a book that shares his worldview: Aldous Huxley's *Brave New World*. It came out four years ago in English, and in German under the title *Whither the World?* Roth regularly gets on the nerves of the rest of the circle by reading aloud quotes from the book about how surveillance will be the norm in the world of the future. "The embryo factory! The new man! Sexually mature at four, fully grown at six and a half! A triumph of science!" Roth's laugh is bitter, and he keeps returning to the same passages.

"Sepp! Enough! We know already!" Kisch tries to check him. "Your Huxley's a reactionary amateur! Chaplin's the genius of our time!" And now Kisch takes the floor. He recounts his visit to Chaplin, when the latter showed him every film in his private screening room that Kisch had never seen before, and laid his hand on Kisch's knee in the half-darkness of the screening room and searched his face for signs of approval and enthusiasm. "How insecure he was, and proud at the same time," cries Kisch, and then talks about Chaplin's new masterpiece, *Modern Times*, which most of the group have already seen in Paris. But not Roth, of course. The moment Kisch started in about it again, he pulled a face. The cinema is the anti-Christ! The devil! "*Modern Times*—doesn't make me laugh!" he sneers. But Kisch refuses to be provoked, talks about the feeding machine on the assembly line, and acts out Charlie, as he calls him, falling into the machine or leaping, in his swimming trunks, into the shallow water. It's Kisch's star turn. The group in the Flore is almost flat on the floor with laughter. Even the corners of Roth's mouth twitch.

Roth hates the cinema, even if he keeps encouraging Zweig to get an American agent to handle the movie rights to his books. He needs the money, and nobody pays more, or faster, than Hollywood. They've already filmed *Job*.* Roth hasn't seen it but Zweig has told him about it and now reports to the whole circle that the movie ver-

*The American title of the film was *Sins of Man*.

sion is a scream. The story has simply been turned into an American melodrama. "You have to see it, Roth! You won't recognize a thing! But it's hilarious!" "No, I won't."

That's how the evening goes. One bottle of Verveine du Velay follows another. The mood is boisterous but also strained. You have the feeling that one wrong word, and the whole table would explode. Kisch keeps up his lecture on *Modern Times* for a bit: the hero isn't Charlie, of course, the hero is/are the modern times themselves, the exploitation of the workers, the universal surveillance, American capitalism as the enemy. Then they talk about the general strike in France and Belgium. Here at the seaside you notice almost nothing, but the country is crippled. A hundred thousand people have stayed away from work for weeks; in France it began at the beginning of June. "They're going to triumph!" cries Kisch. Vacation entitlement, a forty-hour week, higher pay—it really looks as if the concerted power of the unions will force the state and the industrial concerns to their knees. "Paid vacation! What do you think is going on in summer here?" cries Kesten. "We can hardly get around in all this vacation mob as it is." Roth and Zweig and the women laugh. Kisch finds it less funny and tells Kesten to keep his cynicism to himself. There'll always be room somewhere for him and his stomach.

Now Kesten is insulted. His stomach is nobody's business but his, and as far as he's concerned, every Frenchman and every Belgian can take their vacation here, so long as Thomas Mann doesn't show up. This unites everyone in mocking agreement. At the beginning of the month Mann had arranged for a speech to be read out at the European Amnesty Conference in Brussels. The speech, they all agree, wasn't bad. It was clear and urgent. An appeal to those in power in Germany to open the gates of the prisons and let all political prisoners go. Then he added that the world would then recognize that Germany was governed by spiritual values, not by despotism. "He's absolutely mad! What spiritual values?" asks Toller. They resent Thomas Mann for taking so long to make himself one of the exiles, for trying not to wreck things with the regime in Germany, and for not wanting to lose the German market. Everyone here lost it long ago. The last to do so was Stefan Zweig, who is the only one not joining in the mockery. It is Joseph Roth who relays the rumor that Mann has been identified as a Jew in a report about the congress, and has formally denied it publicly. What a coward! And Roth says that the author of *The Magic Mountain*, whose concern is always balance and neutrality, simply bears the wrong name. "'Man'—what an error. I've only ever seen him as an 'It.'"

Then they get incensed about the closing of the exiles' most important German-language daily newspaper, the *Pariser Tageblatt*, which happened on June 14. How few publishing venues remain where they can appear in their native language. There has been a long-running conflict between the publisher and financial backer Vladimir Polia-kov and the editorial staff, most particularly the editor in chief, Georg Bernhard, who had been the editor in chief of the *Vossische Zeitung* in the Weimar Republic. Bern-hard and the editorial staff accused the publisher of secret collaboration with the National Socialists. They left the paper in a body and founded a new one, the *Pariser Tag-eszeitung*. Everyone here in Ostend and also the émigrés in Paris know that the accusation is absurd. A committee of investigation has been set up to dig into the charges. Everyone knows they'll find nothing. But the newspaper, with its circulation of fourteen thousand, is gone. The new one, which is currently carrying the first serialization of *Mephisto* and also Thomas Mann's speech, must manage without a financial backer. And with measurably fewer readers.

And is there actually bad news? Is it, for example, bad news that the publisher Gottfried Bermann-Fischer has founded a new publishing house in Vienna, leaving the old Fischer Verlag behind in Germany under the leader-ship of Peter Suhrkamp? On July 15 he announced "the founding of a new publishing enterprise to [his] esteemed colleagues in the book trade." Bringing with him all the authors of the old Fischer Verlag who had found themselves to be impossible in Germany, including Alfred Döblin, Alfred Kerr, Jakob Wassermann, Carl Zuckmayer, and, most of all, Thomas Mann. Another exiles' publishing house! More German-language literature for the minuscule market in such books abroad. No, this news doesn't make anyone here particularly happy either.

The mood remains depressed and irritable. Soon the circle is joined by the filmmaker Géza von Cziffra. He travels to and fro between Berlin, Paris, and Brussels. In this atmosphere poisoned by mistrust, he's not the ideal man to bring cheer to the uneasy group. But Kisch likes him, and it's because of Kisch that he's here. Cziffra, like almost everyone else, is busy with a historical project: he's planning a film on the Emperor Maximilian. And Kisch claims he himself is the nephew of the emperor's personal physician. He talks about Emperor Franz Joseph's fantastical plan to have his brother Archduke Maximilian crowned emperor of Mexico, to encourage him to give up all the rights of an Austrian archduke. Roth listens with interest but with mounting disbelief. Then he's had enough: "Stop spreading this mad story, Egonek! Franz Joseph would never have done any such thing against his own brother!" "Well, perhaps not against his brother," Kisch replies, but he knows that Maximilian in reality is a grandson of Napoleon, who had a secret relationship with Archduchess Sophie, the wife of Archduke Franz Karl.

Roth freezes, looks in horror at his friend, screams, "Disgusting, disgusting three times over" into his face, jumps to his feet, and stumbles out without saying goodbye. Irmgard Keun hurries after him. The whole circle of the émigrés comes back to life, slowly shaking off the shock, and they disappear wordlessly and soft-footed into the night.

．．．

IRMGARD KEUN LOVES JOSEPH ROTH and sees into him more deeply than anyone ever has. She knows that the two of them have come together this summer primarily out of loneliness, and she loves this loneliness and sadness in him, and his desire to have her always and totally and completely at his side. At night, when they're next to each other in bed, he sometimes plunges his hands deep, deep into her hair, as if afraid that she might suddenly disappear in the darkness. And in the morning, after she's slowly disentangled her hair from his small, white hands, she holds his head when he needs to vomit, for hours. Meanwhile she's read all his books. He hasn't read any of hers. But he drives her to write, unceasingly. In a letter to Arnold Strauss she says that she and Roth engage every day in "the purest literary Olympics." She works at warp speed, and yet when they count their pages in the evenings, he usually has more than she does. If she's tired, doesn't want to get up, doesn't want to go to the bistro and write, he won't let her get away with it. She's not a woman, she's a soldier, a writer with a mission in the world. No time out to relax, no breaks. Writing is a sacred duty. Breaks are a sin, in his eyes. It's the law by which he leads his life. Irmgard Keun is prepared to live under this law, for a while.

She loves his gift of being able to laugh at himself, at his clumsy awkwardness as a soldier and his unheroic life. But she soon learns that this in no way means that she is allowed to repeat these stories later and laugh. He is enormously vulnerable, even oversensitive, and not even Irmgard Keun can guess what will upset him. "He was so easily wounded that he had to wear a mask even with me," she tells Roth's biographer David Bronsen in later years.

The way she sees him is that he is the same in personal matters and in small things as he is in political matters and in the big things. His understanding is clear and acute, and he sees everything exactly, both his own downfall and the downfall of his world, and of course he also sees that his monarchism is a chimera, a childish belief, a sweet lie that he tells himself day after day to make life and his own clarity and knowledge endurable. It is why one becomes a writer, to see the world another way and wish it into otherness, to describe it as other than it is and will become.

Irmgard Keun knew everything about Roth: "In his books Roth loved to submerge himself in the world of the old Austrian monarchy—a world that he made the most despairing and fervent efforts to believe was—at least once in the past—the home of all thought and all feeling. But he knew that he had no home, and never would have one.

Everything that came near him—people, things, ideas—he recognized in all their most hidden inadequacies, and he detected the cold that can freeze even the warmest living breath. So he searched out worlds that were completely foreign to him, and that he hoped would remain warmer and less recognizable. But no matter how successful his eternally creative fantasies, they were always undone by his furious intelligence. He would have blessed the devil and hailed him as god if he had helped him to believe. From time to time he saw himself in some ghostly empty space between the rational and the mystical, untethered from reality and unable to reach the unreachable, knowing too that it was indeed unreachable. He was tortured and wanted to be free of himself and able in any circumstances to be something that he was not."

It comes most easily when he's writing. "Bunny, I've got a beautiful invention," he calls over to his girlfriend at her table. He flashes a smile and has already vanished into his invention again. Much that he writes is drawn directly from things he sees here and that they discuss. And after he's written it down, Irmgard Keun can barely recognize them again: "His lightning-quick fantasy had transformed them into something else." And he always has good ideas, not just literary ones but practical ideas for living. When Irmgard Keun complains that she doesn't know how to extract a divorce agreement from her Nazi supporter of a husband in Germany, who's fighting it, Roth suggests she simply send him a postcard saying she's in Belgium sleeping with Negroes and Jews, and the whole thing will settle itself. Roth likes thinking up ideas and always believes that he owes the best ones to schnapps. "If you want, I'll show you the good places in each of my books that I owe to a fine Calvados," he once said to Soma Morgenstern. Unfortunately he didn't have his books at hand when he said it.

What he likes to do best with his girlfriend is making things up. He has such beautiful long eyelashes, she once says to him. To which he says yes, he knows—it comes from the fact that he once had an eye infection long ago that blinded him briefly, and all his eyelashes had to be plucked out. During this incident he had to keep walking around in a whole troupe of blind men and sometimes banged into walls. This doesn't precisely explain why his eyelashes grew back so thick and long as a result, but it's a good story.

Stefan Zweig likes to tell a tale about a memory, in spring some years back, of meeting the beautiful wife of a publisher. "How well this beautiful May morning suits Frau Kiepenheuer" was his charming salute. To which Roth added, "You haven't yet seen her on a September evening." To which Zweig, outdone, says, "Now we know what a great writer you are."

Joseph Roth is always at his most charming when Irmgard Keun least expects it. She says, without thinking, that she misses German black bread here. Then Roth sees a dray horse being fed black bread by its owner. Roth follows man and horse for long enough to reappear in front of his girlfriend half an hour later, beaming with joy and clutching a slab of black bread.

When they write—and they're almost always writing—Keun and Roth sit at separate tables, she at the window, he right at the back of the bistro. He can't stand the sun. His eyes, his swollen feet, his skin, his suit—nothing about the man is made for the summer sun. They sit within calling distance of each other. Each of them watching the other mistrustfully to see who's getting on faster. And who's drinking more.

Their shared writing day begins by reading the horoscope in *Paris Soir* and ends at five p.m. with the arrival of Stefan Zweig. He goes past her little table with a short pause to say hello, and into the dark corner in the back, where his friend is.

At the beginning when they first meet, Irmgard Keun keeps her distance, writing to America: "Stefan Zweig is a fine man, as smooth as velvet, dripping with goodwill and love of his fellow men. I can't begin to cope with either him or his books." The two of them are utterly foreign to each other. But there's something else: jealousy of this man who has taken on something of the role of a faithful, concerned wife in the chaotic life of Joseph Roth. And shame as well. She doesn't want to see her beloved writer dependent on this man. She doesn't want Zweig to be allowed to feel superior to Roth. She doesn't want her brilliant Roth to allow himself to be kept by Zweig. Gradually all this develops into something close to enmity, and she soon sees Roth's best friend with hostile eyes. "He seems very decorative. Just the way a cinemagoer would imagine a famous writer. Worldly, elegant, well groomed, and a touch of gentle melancholy in the eyes. He talked with loving sincerity about Vienna and painted charming pastel pictures of his life, which has already begun its quiet, unstoppable descent into decay."

If Roth makes fun of Zweig, it's in self-defense, out of an effort to retain his self-respect, not to lose it here, in his new suit, paid for by his great friend. Every day he wears it on his own body. This gift, this symbol of his inferiority in the world of money. Joseph Roth writes about it in his books. The glitter, the necessity of money, and how simple life is in a world where the money never runs out and the idiots out there give the narrator the respect he has earned.

It's also in the book he's just finished, the second half of which he's revising again in the dark corner of the Belgian bistro: *Confession of a Murderer*. It's the story of Golubchik, who grows up fatherless and dirt poor somewhere in the forests of Joseph Roth's homeland. His apparent father is the rich, distant, passionate Prince Krapotkin, who knows nothing of this son, the fruit of a long-forgotten affair, nor wants to find out. Golubchik fights his entire life for recognition, becomes a pitiless informant for the Russian secret police, falls for the glorious Lutetia, follows her to Paris, loves money, is addicted to display and to new clothes: "I needed all those available external validations: clothes for myself and Lutetia, the subservience of the tailors who took my measurements in the hotel with careful fingers, as if I were a fragile idol; who barely mustered the courage to touch my shoulders and my legs with the tape. Because I was merely a Golubchik, I needed everything that would have been a burden to a Krapotkin: the hangdog look in the eye of the porter, the servile backs of the waiters and servants, of whom I got to see no more than their perfectly shaved necks. And money, I needed money too."

It is Stefan Zweig with whom he revises the second half of the *Confession* one more time. He reads it out loud to him and gives his friend the pages of the first draft. The collaboration with Zweig leads to so many revisions that Roth has to write from Ostend to his publisher Walter Landauer that after page sixty-five a great deal has been altered, that the most important changes are contained in the last two galleys and the end has been totally rewritten. He doesn't write to whom he owes these alterations but adds that Stefan is there too and would love to see Landauer. Roth knows how important the best-selling and well-connected Zweig is for Landauer and the notoriously hard-up publishing house of Allert de Lange, and he drops the possibility of such a meeting into his letter casually, calculatedly offhand. Landauer hurries to respond: "It would be good if I could speak to Herr Stefan Zweig this coming Wednesday."

It is unlikely that Stefan Zweig has time for Walter Landauer that very Wednesday. At the seaside this summer he seems to have time for nothing. Or rather, for everything. He gets hardly any mail, which is to say almost no bad news, no begging letters, no attacks either because of *Castellio* or his abandoned wife and the abandoned house on the Kapuzinerberg, no attacks because of his excessive political caution, and none because of any excessive aggression. He wants peace, here in the north in his ideal summer place, just peace, not for himself but for his work.

What was it he'd written to Lotte? "We'd live simply there." But in the same letter he'd added who—or what—he was also expecting to accompany this simple living by the seashore: "You and the machine." Perhaps a little heartless in a letter to his still-secret lover, when he wrote at the end of June that he would be in touch with her by telegram "so that you and the machine can arrive one or two days later."

And when he sent on his written travel instructions to Lotte in London from Ostend on July 3, he repeated under point four what was to be brought with her: "The machine of course." Zweig's chief desire was to work. So he would be followed not just by his secretary and lover Lotte Altmann but also by his friend and editor Emil Fuchs, who had promised to come, and arrived from Salzburg a few days ago to help Zweig put together the second volume of novellas, which is due to be published by his new publishing house, Reichner, in the fall.

Fuchs is Zweig's longtime editor; a close working friendship has developed over the years, and the two men share a silent passion: chess. But in the evenings, if Zweig isn't sitting with Roth, he's usually with Fuchs for hours, smoking cigars, silent in front of a chessboard.

. . .

So Zweig has an entire writing office here, and he's working better and more effectively than he's done for years. Fuchs works on the volume of novellas more or less independently while Zweig writes two of the miniatures for a new edition of *Shooting Stars*, one about the conquest of Byzantium, the other about Lenin's journey through Germany to Russia in the sealed train in 1917.

Both of them come easily to him. He's collected all the basic materials already, and the history of Byzantium is a kind of by-product of the big story he's writing at the moment, and for which, more than ever, he's relying on help from Joseph Roth. "I'm working on this novella," he'd written to Roth two months before leaving for Ostend. "It's really a legend, a Jewish legend, which I've built up both high and wide over a very narrow historical foundation. I think it's going to be good, despite my reluctance to say such things. But I'm not so sure about the style. Which is why I need you to look at it." But the style is not the only thing Zweig is unsure about in this instance. It's the religious or, more accurately, the ritual aspect. At the end of June he writes to Roth: "It would be my good fortune to have you in place as my literary conscience for this legend. We could test ourselves together of an evening and teach each other the way we did in the good old days." The novella that Zweig is writing will later appear under the title of *The Buried Candelabrum*. It's the legend of a seven-branched candelabrum that wanders from Jerusalem to Babylon, returns, is brought to Rome by Titus, is stolen by the Vandals, then is taken to Carthage and finally is returned to Byzantium. Until Justinian brings it back to

Jerusalem, although to a Christian church, at which point the candelabrum disappears forever. It is the story of the eternal Jewish wanderings that Stefan Zweig wants to continue and complete in Ostend. The story of the menorah, as the story of the Jews' banishment and homelessness and their undying hope that one day there will be an end to the eternal wandering. As he wrote to Roth, he could write only about the things "that are relevant to the times and that provide some kind of reinforcement." Yet it is fundamentally a story of hopelessness and sadness. The candelabrum is lost again and again. Zweig tells the story from the perspective of the Jew Benjamin Marnefesh, who as a boy is a silent and despairing witness to the first act of theft, when the Vandals' slaves take the treasures of Rome on board their ships. In his attempt to snatch the menorah away from one of the slaves, his arm is shattered, he falls, and the menorah seems lost forever. "White foam ran over the keel, it slid forward with a hissing murmur, its brown frame was already rising and falling on the waves as if it were a living, breathing thing, and the galleon, under full sail, steered a straight course out from the roads into the endless expanse of the open sea."

Benjamin Marnefesh will be an old man when his fate and that of the menorah achieve their conclusion. It is roughly at the end of the first third of the book that the Jews of Rome gather at their cemetery on the ninth day of

Av, the day of the destruction of the temple, to read from the *Kinim*, the songs of Lamentation, to pray together, to mourn and remember the day when the world's Jews lost their homeland. At the end of this day the Jews will learn that the candelabrum has been stolen again and has been dispatched to Byzantium. Only one person will smile gently at this news: Benjamin, the most cultivated man in the congregation, senses that this bad news may conceal the kernel of its very opposite.

This passage defeats Stefan Zweig, perhaps because he lacks perspective, or his own personal memories, or experience, or participation, or historical material.

Zweig goes with Roth to Almondo, the Italian restaurant in Langestraat where he manages repeatedly to persuade him to eat. The host, Joseph Almondo, is proud of his two guests, and always serves them himself. And after they've eaten, they all drink a schnapps, a Verveine, together, to aid the digestion, as Almondo always remarks, to the joy of Joseph Roth.

In the afternoons Zweig can occasionally persuade Roth to sit for a while out on the terrace of the bistro with him and Lotte, in the fresh air, the wind, and the sun. Lotte has her camera with her; she laughs and asks the two friends to move together for a moment just this once, for a photo. Basically it's enough for Roth to have put up with the sun shining on his head, but he doesn't really want to put up a fight on such a beautiful day. So he peers into Lotte's lens looking rather skeptical, not to say almost truculent, and lifts his right eyebrow a little in mockery. He's not vain, he doesn't care that the hair on his forehead is thin and a little disheveled or that his colorfully striped bowtie is a little crumpled. His new black jacket sits perfectly. But what to do with his hands? Uncertainly he holds on to the table, lays his hand with its nicotine-yellow fingers still clutching the tail end of a cigarette next to a half-full glass of wine, while Zweig slides over closer to his friend. His chair is somewhat higher, which makes him half a head taller than Roth; he smiles at him self-confidently. Zweig, whose tweed suit, waistcoat, and tie are making him too hot on this summer day, pays no attention to the camera but looks at Roth. Lotte sees Zweig's look through the lens; yes, he's looking down at his friend, but it is a fatherly look, or a big brother's, gentle, loving, a little concerned. He sits there with a benevolent smile, and in Lotte's camera it looks as if he'd have liked to put his arm around his friend's shoulders, while Roth looks as if such a protective gesture is exactly what he fears.

Lotte takes her photo. Roth relaxes again, they talk about the day's work more intensively and concisely than they have for a long time, in the way that they can do with nobody else. And Zweig tells Roth his problem with the

Jewish legend and the passage that he just can't get right. Such a thing is only possible with a relative, a brother, someone whose every line you know, someone whose old books you know, just as you know his new plans. "Terrible fate of a people, who must always wait for 'tomorrow' and 'perhaps,' always trust mutely in the written word and never receive a sign!" Zweig writes. And what was it like on the day of deepest mourning in the month of Av? What was that like, Roth?

. . .

In the evenings, everyone goes their own way again, Roth to the Hôtel de la Couronne to Irmgard Keun—Zweig has given him money so that he can pay for his room weeks in advance—and Zweig back to his small apartment in the Maison Floréal by the sea, on the broad Albert I promenade, a beautiful dark corner house with a little tower. He lives on the fourth floor, Lotte on the fifth, and there's no elevator. Yes, it was barbaric for her, he had written to her beforehand, but that was the only way it would function. He needs his loggia—a workroom with a view of the sea and infinity. As Benjamin had seen it as a boy, watching the candelabrum disappear and wanting to save it: "He stared as if spellbound at the sea, which he espied for the first time. There it was, an endless mirror of blue, radiantly vaulted as far as the sharp divide where the waters met the sky and this enormous space seemed to him to be the dome of night, for it was the first time he had seen the full arch of the stars in the hollow of the heavens."

So Zweig can look out at the North Sea every day and every evening. The lights of the casino shine all the way up into his room, making the sea in front of him all the darker.

Early next morning, a letter from Roth arrives, a little scrap of paper, only a few lines on it. A love letter, written in the course of the previous night. "Dear good friend," it says, "in the manner of teenage girls and schoolboys, I have to tell you how sweet you were to me today, with the hotel and everything, and so I'm telling you, the way I would have said it at the age of eighteen when I tried in vain to find you in your apartment in Vienna. I'm thanking you for a piece of my youth and the capacity for sweet senseless talk. This time I'm giving you something written. Your J.R."

His visit to Zweig's house, where he had stood outside as a worshipful student—perhaps last night was the first time Roth had ever told his friend that story. How he stood there to no avail in a waistcoat, tie, and high white collar. It was only thirteen years later that Stefan Zweig became aware of his young colleague when Alfred Beierle, the skilled public speaker, gave him Roth's book *The Wandering Jews*, the history of the Jews of eastern Europe who come to the West and are regarded there as a "problem," as "guests from the East," somewhat embarrassing relatives of the assimilated western Jews, poor and most of them recognizable at first glance as Jews.

It was the history of the world Joseph Roth himself came from, of the situation of the Jews of the Soviet Union, of the emigration to America: "Many emigrate out of some kind of urge, without really knowing why. They follow a vague call of the wild, or the specific call of a relative who's already there. They have a yearning to see the world and to escape the supposed confines of their homeland, the will to be effective and have their strengths amount to something.

"Many return. More stop somewhere along the way. The Eastern Jews have no home, but they have graves in every cemetery. Many become rich. Many become important. Many become creative in a foreign culture. Many lose themselves and their purchase on the world. Many remain in the ghetto, and it is only their children who will eventually leave it again. The majority give to the West at least as much as they take from it. But all of them have the right to live in the West, at least all of them who sacrifice themselves to get there."

Zweig, the western Jew, was so moved by this book that

he wrote a letter to Joseph Roth to thank him for it and for his writing.

It was the beginning of their friendship, because Joseph Roth did not just thank his long-admired hero for the letter, he was ready with an immediate contradiction: "I don't agree with you when you say that the Jews don't believe in a hereafter. But that is a debate that would require a great deal of time and space."

The envelope that reaches Stefan Zweig this morning contains not only the little piece of notepaper but a sheet filled with writing but with no header. It's the "written" thing that Roth mentioned in his letter thanking Zweig for his friendship. It begins: "On the day of the ninth of Av the Jews gathered in the cemetery, as religious tradition demanded. Some read from the 'Kinim,' the songs of Lamentation. Every word therein was salty and bitter, like a tear." Roth writes about the graves, the inscriptions on the graves, and about one gravestone into which the menorah had been carved: "which signifies that under this stone were rotting the bones of a Jew who once had gone through life with a wise heart, careful hands, a lucid mind, a sure tread, clear-eyed, had felt the world, thought it, understood it, seen it, and walked all through it. He had been a true light in Israel, which is why the candelabrum lighted his grave." It is also a text about the touch of pain felt by the congregation as they watch the ninth day of Av slowly draw to its end. And he concludes: "People were already closing the books, already beginning to think about their departure. Suddenly they heard the soft, melancholy creak of the old cemetery gate. Who might have left or come? The gate had been closed!"

Stefan Zweig reads and reads and is filled with deep gratitude. It is the text he has failed to write, the hinge, the day of deepest mourning in the Jewish cemetery in Rome between the overturned gravestones, before the gate opens and the messenger brings news that the menorah has been stolen again. Roth has written it for him, and Stefan Zweig inserts it into his legend, alters the tone and the melody a little, changes it into his text about the Jewish congregation of Rome, "as they gathered in the cemetery according to their custom, on the most grievous day of their year, the ninth day of Av, the day of the destruction of the temple, that day of grim memory that rendered their fathers homeless and scattered like salt across all the lands of the earth." He writes about gravestones that announce "that he who lies here in eternal slumber, was a wise man and himself a light in Israel." And finally, about the end of the day: "They did not notice that the ninth of Av, the day of deep mourning, was slowly drawing to a close and the hour was approaching of the last prayer. Then, outside, the rusty gate of the cemetery creaked."

It will become in some small way their shared book, the story of eternal flight and of the belief that there is a place, which will hold its secret forever, where the Jews of the world will be able to live in peace. Benjamin has a replica of the menorah made; it is stolen again, disappears somewhere, but he has other plans for the genuine one: "God must decide, he and only he, the fate of the candelabrum. I will bury it, I know of no other way to truly protect it, but for how long, who can tell! Perhaps God will leave it forever in darkness, and our people will have to wander comfortless, dusty, and scattered over the back of the earth. Yet perhaps—and my heart is filled with this faith—perhaps his will may decree that our people go home to their land." And then Zweig adds—and perhaps this is a real return to his friend Roth and his belief in the hereafter: "Do not concern yourself with the decision, leave it to him and to time! Let the candelabrum be presumed lost. We, we who are God's secret—we are not lost! For gold does not disappear into the lap of the earth like the earthly body and our people do not disappear into the darkness of time. One will endure and the other will endure, our people and the candelabrum! So let us believe that that which we bury will rise again and light the people, the homecomers. For only if we do not cease to believe will we withstand the world."

It's an entreaty that Zweig is writing here with Roth's

assistance. An entreaty born of faith and a hope for an end to flight, including their flight—Zweig's, Roth's. That of their entire circle here at the shore. What will happen after the summer? It is slowly reaching its end.

As Roth had written in his text for Zweig: "It was already very late in the summer, it was already a very old, very tired summer, shortly before the fall. Summer itself resembled an old Jew, summer itself seemed to want to rest in the graveyard. It was mild, good-natured, and of golden wisdom."

. . .

A few days later they are all sitting together again. All burned brown, except for Roth, the old enemy of sunshine. They are sitting in the Flore once more, with its view of the sea and the little bathing huts. Christiane Toller knits away defiantly, Gisela Kisch laughs whenever there's something to laugh about and even when there isn't. Lotte Altmann is quiet, and it's only when she coughs softly that the rest of the circle even notices she's still there. Emile Fuchs looks at the sea. Stefan Zweig sits between Lotte and Fuchs, smoking and listening as Egon Kisch talks about Spain, the war of the Communists, the latest reports from the front, and Arthur Koestler about his travel plans, which should bring him into Franco's headquarters. Ernst

Toller blazes away at him, admittedly only half-seriously, but all the more loudly, merrily, and determinedly. Kesten laughs along with Gisela Kisch at the heatedness of the men, Christiane's knitting, and Stefan Zweig's silence. Irmgard Keun has fetched Joseph Roth out of the dark corner of the bistro into the light, drinks with him, and whenever he casts a brief, sarcastic remark into the circle, she seems for a moment to hesitate. She would so love to be on the side of the Communist believers, and also on the side of the harmless, somehow uninvolved laughing audience. But she's with him, and his lack of belief is hers too, even if she knows that his religion, his monarchism, is just another form of escape, a trapdoor that is not open to her. There are laughter, argument, and things unspoken this evening at the Café Flore, but everything is more muted than at the beginning of the summer. Hope has melted a little further. Despite Spain. Because of Spain. Despite the German-Austrian agreement or because of it. And despite the peace in Germany and in Berlin in advance of the Olympics. Another summer is passing without the arrival of the decisive turning point, without real signs that the Fascist domination in Europe is approaching its end. At least not this summer, not this year, and for many people no longer within the time frame they will live to see.

· · ·

"I'M AS BLACK AS A NEGRO," Erwin Kisch writes to his mother in Prague shortly before he leaves, then he travels back to Versailles with Gisela; next summer he will set off for Spain to join the war. Arthur Koestler meanwhile has already gone in the same direction. Ernst Toller, to Christiane's horror, has accepted an invitation to do a lecture tour across America. She had accepted a one-year theater engagement in London, an extraordinary chance for a young German actress in exile. "Please no!" she begs him. "You have to stay home!" "Home? Where's that?" asks Toller in reply. And in October she stands on the deck of the SS *Normandie*, salt water in her face, hoping that the wind will blow her back to England and London instead of New York, according to plan. But it doesn't blow hard enough.

Hermann Kesten is struggling with his *Philip II* and is failing to make progress. The advance from the publishing house is used up; he wants to stay in Amsterdam near the publishing house and write and live halfway cheaply. Then a new edict is issued that refugee identity cards will become mandatory in Holland. So in October he goes to

Paris again, to apply for this identity card, but he no longer has enough money for the return journey. From the train he writes to a friend: "At every station boys get on, heading for the garrison, at every station the same family stands, weeping mother, melancholy father, giggling sister; they wave as if the son were already going off to a kind of prelude to war."

Stefan Zweig and Lotte Altmann also leave the summer resort. Zweig is happier than he's been for years. Filled with inspiration, he writes to Friderike—with whom he's done nothing in the last months but fight, in person and by letter—about his happiness here in Belgium; his work, which has advanced so well, better than it has in a long time; the peace, the absence of arguments and bad reviews. "And I've managed to lift Roth as well, he eats something every day now—though nobody can compel him to take a walk, let alone go for a swim. I also took care of him for a time, though I feel things look black for him—as they do for all writers —; sales are plummeting and the difficulties are only going to increase." And he's just had a wonderful swim and hopes to have another, his last tomorrow morning early.

Before he leaves, however, he walks down a cul-de-sac that leads away from the sea, rising toward the town. The narrow house is still there. The window display is the same as it was, shells suspended on threads, grinning masks, starfish, ashtrays. But it's obviously no longer a shop. James Ensor is a famous man, the king of Ostend; he's been made a baron, and since the death of his mother, the entire house has become his atelier. Stefan Zweig hesitates over whether to go in and upstairs to the skull wearing the lady's hat, the man at the piano, and the thousand spite-filled masks behind. He doesn't. He turns back toward the sea. One last swim.

Saying goodbye to Roth is both hard, for Zweig, and easy. It's freeing. His burden, the most beloved weight on his shoulders, his bad conscience, his literary conscience, his incorruptible, difficult friend is staying behind, while he himself is starting out for a new world. Yes, he lifted him up, has left money for him, and brought order to his contracts, even some order into his life. And now there's Keun here too, who makes Roth happy, who looks after him, is by his side and will stay there, untroubled by all the destructiveness and the self-destructiveness, maybe even spurring it on with her furious urge to live, to write, to drink. With her love of him, of his hatreds, his sadness, his readiness to go down in flames if the world cannot be saved. Zweig is leaving Roth with his lover.

The evening before his departure, they are at their Italian restaurant yet again, one street below the promenade;

one last good burst of encouragement from Zweig, one last discussion of plans, literary plans. One last Verveine. Zweig wants to believe he's leaving his friend with future prospects that are halfway stable, so he can leave without feeling pity. But deep inside he knows quite clearly that the stabilization that has taken place this summer is no more than a little false security. He has written to Huebsch that Roth's novels are getting worse, and things look black for him and his books, both in the European market and in America. Zweig knows this and doesn't want to know it. He can't do any more for Roth without being dragged under himself. Not now. He wants to be free. The summer has given him new strength in a way few summers have done. He's determined to make use of this new surge of energy for a kind of breakthrough. He believes in it again and is set on retaining that belief.

It's back to London with Lotte, and then from there to Southampton, where on August 8 he will set sail for Brazil, alone, without Lotte, without Friderike, without Roth, without Fuchs.

From his homeland, from the old house on the Kapuzinerberg, comes one last piece of news. It's Festival time, as it is every year. Toscanini is there, along with Bruno Walter. They are putting on an anti-Bayreuth, a not-Nazi German festival of theater and music. A demonstration.

But Zweig is glad not to be there. He has always hated the hurly-burly at the Festival and tried to avoid his city during this period. Despite his love for Toscanini and his world. On the last day at the shore in Belgium, he writes to a friend in Salzburg: "You know how the atmosphere there has weighed on me so dreadfully for years now. I was completely undone by it and couldn't work. To add to that were the conflicts you know about with my close family who were forever condemning my so-called pessimism and wanting to bind themselves closer to me out of nostalgia to the very degree that I was struggling to get out. I am almost forgetting those glorious years that I wasted there because of the bitterness I suffered. In the last years it was a secret and ever-increasing source of pleasure for me to feel that the world of Toscanini was living its last. It was, and indeed is again this year, as beautiful as a sunset."

And now mail has arrived out of this sunset, from the house still occupied by the very members of the family who had condemned his pessimism, Friderike and her daughters. They loved to act as its representatives, and during every Festival it was always filled with a crowd of guests—which this year included Klaus Mann and his sister Erika. Klaus sent a postcard to the master of the house, innocent, carefree, brief: "Greetings! You should envy us! Your house is enchanting. Why aren't you here? How can it be more beautiful in Rio or Ostend?" The previous day this same Klaus Mann had written in his diary: "In between all the toing-and-froing: constant *severe* attacks of sadness. Before I go to sleep I always imagine my death. Who will sit there at my bedside? No one?—I think of a string of words: 'But an angel will have mercy on me.'" And two days later: "Rain. Everyone still asleep. I can't sleep that long. Vomit in the bathroom. . . . I think of all the parties I've been to . . . the lost faces."

Tears in the diary, merriment on the postcards, and laborious efforts to arouse envy. Back straight. Never show weakness. Not to enemies and not to friends. "Your house is enchanting." While thinking about death. The writer Annette Kolb is also in Salzburg this year. She too senses that she's probably seeing it all for the last time. "The knowledge of events in the world, the hopelessness, weighed on our mood. The hellish emanations from the war in Spain reached the lakes, the forests, and even the concert halls." A gentle wave of farewell: "Who told her she would return to Salzburg? Is life not becoming more and more uncertain from year to year?" And she ends her Salzburg book with the words "Beautiful, endangered Austria, farewell once more! Heart of Europe, commended to God."

This pessimism has been rooted deep and unbudgingly in Zweig's soul for years. Now, as the shadows are falling, he draws strength from what he wrote in his final letter from Ostend to his friend in Salzburg: "The very fact that I'm inclined à la longue to pessimism gives me a certain heightened capacity for enjoyment; we should take every good thing with us, for as long as we can enjoy it."

. . .

It's a happy man who boards the ship at Southampton, although the decor is less appealing: "Crude ostentation, no sense of style," he remarks in his diary. "The weather wonderfully calm and with a September coolness." The goal of his journey is Argentina, where he is to speak as the Austrian representative at the PEN Writers' Congress. But what Zweig really wants from this trip is to try out a new life, to test whether a life would be possible for him there, for him and also for Lotte. The two of them had been learning Spanish together in the last weeks; now here on board he will keep on studying on his own. Stefan Zweig is alone among hundreds of passengers. He savors his aloneness, he's traveling incognito, none of the passengers in first class recognize him; he sees some of them read-ing his books. But when he once goes to the lower decks where the Jews are traveling third class, he's immediately recognized as "the great writer," as he notes proudly in his dairy. "They're happy to have me come visit."

Zweig has begun a new book here on board, a book

about the sympathy that contains good only when it is true sympathy, true fellow-feeling, when the sympathetic person is willing to share the feeling and the suffering to the very end. It's the story of a young officer in the old Austrian army who, out of weakness and soft sympathy, which really is no more than a desire to free himself from the sight of misery, becomes guilty of the death of the sick young woman whom he'd hoped to save by dint of his general benevolence. The story of an officer who eventually will throw himself, almost in relief, into the battles of the First World War, in order to lose himself, and lose his life, while losing his guilt. The book will be called *Beware of Pity*, and it will be Stefan Zweig's only novel. The theme has always preoccupied him; now, in these years of exile, more than ever. Is a life without guilt possible?

Stefan Zweig is a man who can read people like books and therefore doesn't judge them but understands them. Which means that he never wishes to choose between possibilities. A dream: Stefan Zweig is young, perhaps twenty-five years old, soft face, mustache, tiny glasses. He's on board a ship that's supposed to be taking him from Genoa to Naples. He makes friends with one of the humblest waiters, by the name of Giovanni. Before they dock, Giovanni comes to him with a letter. Please, would he read it out loud to him? Zweig doesn't understand. Asks why he doesn't read it himself. He can't—he doesn't know how to read. The traveler can't get his mind around this. His world is a world of books; love, knowledge, thoughts—he has learned all of it from books. He had never thought about it before, but in this moment it dawns on him. A wall separates him from this Giovanni. He doesn't know what he'd be without reading, without books. He can't imagine it. Zweig writes it all down later, in a text with the title *The Book as Entrance to the World:* "And I understood that the gift of the blessing of being able to think in a wide-ranging fashion and amid a multiplicity of connections, that this magnificent ability, the only true way to contemplate the world from a multiplicity of vantage points at once, is only granted to the man who transcends his own experience to absorb from books what they can tell of many lands and peoples and times. I was shattered to realize how narrow a person must find the world if he denies himself books. But moreover, my very thinking about these things, the fact that I could feel as vehemently as I did about what poor Giovanni lacked in heightened pleasure in the world, that gift of being able to be shattered by the chance fate of a stranger, was this not something I owed to my preoccupation with the literary? For when we read, what are we doing if not sharing the inner life of strangers, seeing with their eyes, thinking with their minds? And now, drawing more and more vividly and more and more gratefully on this one moment of happy illumination, I remembered the countless blessings I had received from books. I remembered important decisions I drew from books, encounters with long-dead writers that were more important to me than some with friends and women, nights of love spent with books when you blissfully lost sleep in your enjoyment of them the way you would were you sharing them with another person; and the more I thought about it, the more I realized that our spiritual world is made up of millions of atoms of single impressions, whose minimum number stems solely from what we see and what we experience—while everything else, the existentialist interwoven world, we owe to books, to what is read, transmitted, learned."

Zweig dreamed aboard his ship as it left Genoa. Without books the world remains closed. His world. The way he sees it, the way he's written it in all his books. Sympathy, admiration, living a life without harming others. He even wrote a little story about it, although it passed almost unnoticed. It's called "Anton," and it tells of a man who lives very simply in a small town. A craftsman, someone who can do everything one needs to know how to do in life, who helps people when they need it, who never takes more money than he needs to live at that moment. Who is always disappearing, surfacing when someone needs him. His story ends this way: "For many years I heard no more of Anton. But I can barely imagine anyone about whom there should be less cause for concern: he will never be forsaken by God, and what is even rarer, never by his fellow men."

Stefan Zweig has always openly acknowledged and defended his attempts to stay on the sidelines. Even to those who, he must know, despised him for this stance.

He was still in Ostend when he wrote to his old friend Romain Rolland, whom he loved for his books on music and his pacifism, and who meanwhile has become an ideological Communist, and a Stalinist: "To me the enemy that is dogmatism, of whatever kind, is the one and only ideology that wants to destroy all thought. We need to create a fanatical anti-fanaticism." This he says to Rolland the fanatic and ends, "My dear friend, I think of you so often, for we grow ever more lonely. The word has become weak in the face of brutality, and what we call freedom is incomprehensible to the youth of today: but a new youth will come. And it will understand us!" He has put all his hopes into this letter to his old friend. The reply is short, belligerent, and unambiguous: "No, I am in no way alone or lonely, as you say in your letter. On the contrary, I feel surrounded by the friendship of millions of people from every country and I extend it back to them." The Party writer mocks his lonely friend who doesn't want to take part in the fights of the day. "The words from *Faust* are becoming reality; freedom is being conquered daily on the battlefields of the earth. If I feel lonely anywhere, it's among my fellow writers."

It is much easier to sign on to a movement, an ideology, a party. With what assuredness one can stand on the cliffs of conviction, looking down and mocking the disheartened and the scattered. It is very easy, and no one makes it easier for the ideologues than Stefan Zweig, who so openly articulates his incomprehension of the entire epoch: "Perhaps this is my last great journey, who knows?" he writes in the same letter to Rolland. The Last Journey.

■ ■ ■

It's a little like the way it was back then, in 1914, when he left Ostend on the last train. Stefan Zweig is journeying again into war. Only briefly, yes, only by way of a visit, a port of call. But there's war in Europe again, and out of all the engaged, battle-ready, political colleagues who sat together in Ostend, it's Stefan Zweig, of all people, who is the first to make a stop in Spain. It's August 10, the ship is approaching the Spanish port of Vigo, and there's an American cruiser at the mouth of the bay, which signifies that you go ashore at your own risk. And Zweig goes ashore. He sees "the town full of militia in splendid uniforms, as disciplined as Germans, blue sailor suits, khaki, and helmets. There are thirteen-year-old boys among them, armed with revolvers, hanging around the walls waiting for their pictures to be taken—but I also notice that many of the locals are not wearing the red badge of the Fascists. I watch and photograph heavy trucks packed with helmeted soldiers leaving for the front—they look as vestigially savage as our Home Guard, and it seems, from what I'm told, that even during the fighting the siesta is strictly observed." A flaneur from old Europe on the edge of war. "One could walk around for hours here without realizing that the Front is merely an hour away." And Zweig walks around for hours, watches the cobblers at work, sees his *Maria Stuart* laid out in the windows of the bookshop next to *Hitler's Writings*, Ford's book against the Jews, and "similar nonsense." He sees bewitchingly beautiful people, donkeys, spans of oxen, fast cars, and "old women splendidly reminiscent of Goya with their disheveled, sweaty, dusty hair, dirty feet, and yet a magnificent dignity in their walk." Zweig looks, is astonished, admires, strolls along the edge of the field of slaughter that will be an experimental laboratory for the great war to come, and finds all of it wonderful and picturesque. Two hours of Spain, he writes in his diary with delight, are more intense than a whole year in England. And then the phrase: "like Vienna at that time." Zweig intuits that he's seeing the harbinger of a new world and the eventual collapse of the old one, which is his, or he wouldn't have written that allusion to the Vienna of the old days, but one last time he doesn't want it to be true. One last time he wants to see only beauty, the beautiful people, the good in the world. Spain on the edge of the abyss, happy people, "a piece of magic."

Then back to the open sea, work on the novel, loneliness, and finally—Brazil.

. . .

Stefan Zweig has perhaps never been so overwhelmed in his life, so happy, so proud and confident. How far old Europe lies behind him, and how fast he allows himself to be infected by the enthusiasm of the Brazilians, by the sun, the light, the beaches, and the warmth of the people. A country is lying at his feet. Everyone he meets seems to have read his books. Again and again he writes "wonderful, wonderful" in his diary. In Rio he recognizes the happiest admixture of "Madrid and Lisbon, New York and Paris"; wherever he goes, he's overwhelmed by the enthusiasm of the people, he reads from his books to crowds numbering in the thousands, writes his name hundreds of times each day, is received by the foreign minister and again by the president, receives gifts everywhere, a giant coffee-making machine, the most exquisite coffees, cigars. Having seen his work almost disappear into the darkness of irrelevance, he suddenly draws new courage from this universal goodwill. A whirl of happiness. "Everyone feels that a great future is shaping itself here." And for a few days Stefan Zweig feels it along with them.

And then he decides to take a trip high into the mountains. The old emperor Dom Pedro spent his summers up here when it became unbearably hot down by the sea, at the Copacabana. Zweig wants to see this other city and the emperor's palace, which has become a museum in the meantime, the glass palace on the heights. And he wants to see Brazil, the land, the sea, one time from way up here. A view over the landscape and also a view back toward old Europe. And each day a question hangs unspoken over every step that he takes: is a new life possible here as a continuation of the old one?

Zweig knows already that he can't stay at the seashore, down there in the big city. He cannot cope with the masses of people, the obligations, the claims on him, not at any price. It's a dream of the moment, an enormous source of happiness, to feel that he is loved here in this land of the future the way he is loved nowhere else. But live here, in this dancing metropolis? Out of the question. And an emperor is not the only one for whom the summers are far too hot.

The journey up is also a test. The road keeps climbing, higher and higher. There is a light rain. When you look down: mist. Nature is all-conquering; it is almost impossible to imagine that people can force back the rain forest here. Up at the top, the city runs along the cleft of a valley, green mountains to right and to left, down the middle a narrow brown river, tight paths bordering the road, people bustling around under large umbrellas. The air is glorious, there's no wind, it's fresh and green and damp and pleasantly cool. Stefan Zweig resolved early to love this country. He came here determined to be overwhelmed. He doesn't want to see the dark sides of this new world: the dictatorial regime of President Getúlio Vargas, the expulsion of the Communist Jew Olga Benário Prestes, the anti-Semitic literature of the powerful Fascist movement Brazilian Integralist Action, the restrictive immigration laws. Zweig wants to see none of it. He wants to love.

Back in December 1932 he had already discussed travel plans with his Argentinian translator and agent, Alfredo Kahn. Two weeks in Argentina and then by zeppelin on to Brazil were what was on his mind, and he wrote euphorically, "South America looms ahead of us like a living hope, and we all have a much closer cultural connection to these countries than to North America: the spiritual bond seems to me to be deeper, and besides, it is the New World for us, another sphere."

Political developments in Europe at that time put a stop to his travel plans, but the love for Brazil and South

America was already born in him before he ever set foot in that part of the continent.

And now he's standing here in the drizzle in the mountains of Brazil. No, in truth, not much here recalls the Semmering Pass in his old homeland. But there's the will to remember, the will to rediscover his old world in the new. Does he see the little whitewashed house up here, clinging to the mountainside? And the little garden in front, and the terrace under the overhanging roof? "We would live simply." The Ostend utopia. Is this the place where it will become enduring reality? It's possible.

• • •

JOSEPH ROTH'S AUTUMN THIS YEAR is very different. Stefan Zweig has barely left when misfortune hits him again with full force. First comes a letter from the American publisher Ben Huebsch, informing Roth that he no longer wishes to publish his books. A heavy blow, for the American market is almost the only remaining hope, financially speaking, for German-speaking authors who have emigrated, losing their home audience. Lion Feuchtwanger, Erich Maria Remarque, Thomas Mann, and Stefan Zweig achieve high earnings in the United States, and even Roth's exile publishers in Holland had always been able to calculate licenses in the United States and England as part of their high advances for Roth. After the letter from Huebsch, Roth realizes that for the duration of his exile, he will no longer be able to count on adequate income from his books, no matter how much he writes and no matter how many ideas for novels he sells in parallel to the publishing houses of Allert de Lange, Querido, and De Gemeenschap.

On the very day of Zweig's departure for Brazil, Roth is already sending a letter after him: "I really wanted to write you something cheerful, but alas it's something sad.

Huebsch quite simply fired me." Zweig has been expecting it for some time, but it now becomes clear to him what this could mean for him too: his responsibility, let alone his financial responsibility, for his friend has just increased. And he also realizes that he will be unable to carry it on his own.

At first Roth's panic is contained within bounds. Zweig has left him enough money to be able to live without worries for several weeks. And he hasn't just finished his next novel, *Weights and Measures*, he's already started a new one, *The String of Pearls*. True, both Querido and de Lange turn it down, but De Gemeenschap is ready to pay a not-inconsiderable guarantee of 3,000 guilders, half of which Roth receives as an advance. But that's barely been paid when it is stolen from Roth, who's in Amsterdam with Keun for the negotiations with his publisher, by a young Dutchman, Andreas van Ameringen, who has taken over certain secretarial responsibilities for Roth. The whole advance is gone, along with the money from Zweig. At the same moment Irmgard Keun is arrested for apparent passport violations and is threatened with deportation to Germany. Roth, now completely devoid of means, cannot remain in Holland any longer. Via a stroke of good luck or a friendly official, Keun gets a five-day visa for Belgium and a transit visa for France, and the two of them travel through Brussels and Paris to their eventual destination,

Vienna. Austria has become the only country where Keun can stay without a visa. They live in the Hotel Bristol, where Roth's reputation is still so good that they don't have to pay their bill immediately. For all intents and purposes, neither of them has any money. Allert de Lange refuses for political reasons and for fear of Hitler's Germany to publish Keun's new novel, *After Midnight*, and the two of them keep sending fresh begging letters out into the world. At least old, loyal, besotted Arnold Strauss always sends large sums from America. For a while they live off these.

And just as Stefan Zweig goes through a kind of repeat of his experiences in 1914 with his journey into war and his arrival in a new Vienna, Roth is due a similar trip: "Lemberg still in our possession." The city has long found itself outside the boundaries of Austria. But Roth's relatives still live there, and Roth, who has been invited to make a lecture tour in Poland in the new year of 1937, travels in December 1936 to his old homeland, back to the landscape and people he longs for. In Ostend he bought himself a large haversack that he wanted to take with him when he went wandering, like his Jewish forefathers, as he said to an astonished Keun. He worshiped the pious eastern Jews of his homeland like saints, Keun recalls later; the people of western Europe simply couldn't measure up to their human substance. He has to finally go back to visit them, has to return once more to Galicia. "It's an eternity since I've been there. I have to see it one more time," he says to his friend.

They live in the hotel. Roth doesn't want to live with relatives. "The Jews have such little schnapps glasses," he says.

During the course of this winter of 1936–37, Roth revives. Here and only here, Irmgard Keun says, where he's at home, does he not have to keep playing someone he's not. "Only there, where he came from, was he not splintered into a thousand fragments. He was demonstrably proud of the poorest Jews, like the ones he took me to once, who lived in a cellar where the candles burned even by day. He sat down at their table and spoke Yiddish with them; you could feel the love emanating from him, and I had to love him for it." The only place he doesn't want to go is Brody. "The memories," is Keun's conjecture, "the good as much as the bad, would have been too upsetting for him."

He goes with his cousin Paula Gruebel to the Jewish cemetery, walks along the rows of graves, and says the names of the dead out loud to himself. "A lot of good people lie buried here," he says to Paula.

In *Strawberries*, the fragment of his novel about his homeland, Joseph Roth writes: "I walked along the street that led to the cemetery. I actually intended to go in the opposite direction—to the station. But I must have muddled the directions back then. Perhaps I was thinking that the station wouldn't be opened until morning, whereas the cemetery had to remain open all night. Light was burning in the death chamber. Old Pantalejmon slept there alongside the dead. I knew him, he knew me too. For it was the custom in our town to take walks to the cemetery. Other towns have gardens or parks. We had a cemetery. The children played between the graves. The old people sat on the gravestones and smelled the earth that was made up of our forebears, and was very rich."

Joseph Roth senses that he's seeing it all for the last time. He's "as thin as a skeleton," writes Keun, weighs the same as a ten-year-old boy, only the stomach is like a cannonball. He has only three teeth in his mouth, has heart trouble and pains in his liver, and throws up for hours every day, so that Keun thinks each time he's going to die. He's bad-tempered with her, jealous, never letting her out of his sight for a moment now, and he gets delirious. At night he wakes with a start, calls "Where is Frau Keun?" wildly, and she screams back that they're downstairs in the restaurant, and he should go back to sleep at once. He goes to sleep and remembers none of it the next morning. Arnold Strauss, to whom she describes Roth's symptoms, writes back that his liver won't last more than a year, maximum two.

•••

In the spring of 1937 they're in Salzburg for a few weeks at the invitation of Friderike Zweig, staying in the Hotel Stein at the foot of the Kapuzinerberg. They see Stefan Zweig only briefly. He's as pale as a ghost, chilly. It's the day the sale of his house is being finalized, his final parting from Austria and his previous life. Next day the lawyers in Vienna settle the support payments for his wife and the terms of the separation. Joseph Roth is dreadfully hurt by Zweig's coldness. Where has his old friend gone? He doesn't understand Zweig's unwillingness to see him during these days, or that the problem of Roth is more than he can deal with at this moment. Roth is offended. "You spend more time with assholes than you do with me," he writes from his bit of Salzburg to his friend's. His old savior doesn't reply. In a letter to Lotte, Zweig complains about the "disgustingly drunken Roth." Back in December he had written to Friderike, "What a magnificent man is going to pieces."

Stefan Zweig can no longer help, and no longer wants to. Roth has sensed this for a long time, rages against him, and yet keeps hoping for a happy ending, a return of their wonderful summer. July 1936 all over again, and the sea again, and Ostend.

———

Roth goes. "I want to go to Ostend. It will remind me of you," he writes on July 10, and sets off. Back to the Hôtel de la Couronne, back to the view of the sailboats and the harbor. "Ostend without you. The same bars, and everything's different. Very familiar and very strange. Dreadfully, both at once." He writes letters of longing, love letters. He still hopes that Zweig will come. He asks for money. Zweig sends money. Roth writes about all the friends who've died this summer, for whom he wrote obituaries in the exile papers. But he won't write an obituary for Zweig, so he shouldn't get his hopes up. "You're not just close to me spiritually, but bodily. It's the umbilical cord of friendship: there is such a thing. I don't have the necessary distance from you, the prerequisite for an obituary."

His own death is slow in coming. "The end is dragging on, unfortunately," he writes at the close. "Croaking takes longer than living." And at the foot of the page, after Roth has added "I embrace you," their pasta chef adds his own greeting: "Salutations, Almondo, Ostend." And then Roth adds another line, that Floréal, the owner of the apartment house with the loggia where Zweig stayed, asks after him every day. And absolutely euphoric: "I just met Almondo in the Café Flynt on the square, where I'm writing this. He bought me a bottle of Verveine!!!"

Then the letters become darker and more despairing. Stefan Zweig is not going to come again. One time Roth sees two policemen leading away a suspect. At first he depicts the scene sympathetically, with curiosity, then gets the idea that he could speak to the two officials and alert them to the fact that there's been a mistaken arrest. He himself is the man they're looking for. Roth writes that he hopes this will "avert the definitive catastrophe," but even as he's writing this, he knows that "it's a literary idea" and lets the opportunity pass.

On September 21, sobered, he finally writes, "Dear friend, today I leave. I've waited in vain to see you."

The magical summer resort has brought no change in his life. Roth travels to Paris; here too he hopes to meet up with Zweig again. He pleads, he asks, he makes threats again about his imminent death, he cannot understand why Zweig doesn't make every effort to see him. And at the same time, he knows why; that not even Stefan Zweig can save him anymore. Not with money, not with shared plans, and not with shared books.

. . .

Finally, in February 1938, Stefan Zweig does come to Paris again, with Lotte. They meet. Roth is in catastrophic shape. Irmgard Keun has left him. By the end, he was totally dependent on her, in a panic of jealousy—she couldn't even go out without his mistrust following her. Later, as she remembered it, "in Paris I left him with a deep sigh of relief and went to Nice with a naval officer. I felt as if I'd escaped an unbearable burden."

For almost two years they had been the most remarkable couple among the émigrés, the young old man and the wise woman of the world, the hopeless drinker and the merry imbiber, two fighters pitted against ruin, the ruin of the world and all too soon their own. Irmgard Keun had been dragged deeper and deeper into the whirlpool of disaster. Kisch had been right. Roth had won, she drank and drank and soon could match him, the champion drinker, while preserving a sense of the possibilities, of the two of them maybe finding a way to be good for each other and of mutual assistance. But that was long gone. He clung to her with the last of his strength, pleading like a child. Never has she loved a man as much as him, and she never will again. "My skin said 'yes' at once." As did her soul, everything she had been and still was. But he had slipped through her fingers, grown smaller, paler, more dependent, a wan shadow. In Paris she had to be strong; she had been fearing this moment for a long time. The farewell was brief, unambiguous, spoken at great speed. It was flight—she feared that sympathy would cause her to die along with him. Later she writes about the last meeting in Paris and the parting: "It was like always. It was the end."

But there is still one hope in Joseph Roth's life. In recent months he has paid several visits to the old Austrian emperor-in-waiting, Otto von Hapsburg, in exile in Steenokkerzeel. And the prince, along with Roth and other Austrian monarchists, has dreamed up a desperate plan to propose to the Austrian chancellor, Schuschnigg, that he should resign in favor of the old emperor, thus preventing the threatened annexation of the country to Nazi Germany at the very last moment and saving the fatherland. Otto von Hapsburg writes Schuschnigg a letter laying out the plan, but it's not enough for Roth. Roth is so convinced of the plan that he wants to do everything to put it into action. For him, everything hangs on it. Zweig, whom he tells about it, tries not to cloud his friend's beautiful enthusiasm, but of course he thinks the plan is utter nonsense. Why would Schuschnigg let himself get involved? Why would Hitler let it derail his plans? Zweig too is a dreaming lover of the old Austria, but he sees clearly enough to know that politics is not a fairy tale. Naturally he is troubled when he learns from Roth what Roth's part in the plan is to be, but he doesn't hold him back. He can't save him, nor can he get him to see reason. Roth has finally parted company with the rational world. What is Zweig to do?

Joseph Roth in any case has decided to go to Austria

himself, to win over Schuschnigg to the emperor's plan in person. It is madness. German troops are already at the border, the invasion will start at any moment. And a drunken writer in narrow officer's trousers, which he's started wearing again, is going to stop it?

Yes, that is Roth's plan. Heroically courageous, he says goodbye to Stefan Zweig for the last time. He, who was the first Jewish writer to leave Germany after Hitler seized power, is the last to enter Austria before Hitler seizes power there. He goes by train and has himself announced to the chancellor. But Schuschnigg does not receive Roth. He is merely admitted to see the state secretary for security, Michael Skubl, who has only one message for Roth: *Leave the country as soon as possible. Your life is in the greatest danger.*

On March 11, Joseph Roth journeys back to Paris. On March 12 the Austrian people celebrate the new rulers on the Heldenplatz. Roth's fatherland, and Stefan Zweig's, no longer exists.

. . .

THE FRIENDS NEVER SEE EACH other again. Each takes his own road to death. The distance is not long. Joseph Roth had assured Zweig that he would not write his obituary. He also slowly comes to realize that this temptation will never come within his reach, though he is ten years younger— that his journey will end before Zweig's. But shortly before his death, Roth does write something new about the two of them, a kind of obituary of their friendship, in a book for which Zweig can no longer help him, in neither a literary nor a practical way, nor financially, nor in terms of getting it published. Roth's last book is *The Legend of the Holy Drinker*. A remarkably carefree man staggers around Paris. Homeless, an enthusiastic drinker, and always in big difficulties. He's called Andreas, camps under bridges, and knows that newspapers are good at providing warmth on cold nights. He's on his last legs when a well-dressed man steps into his path one night and presses a large sum of money on him. He calls the unfortunate drinker "brother." The latter replies that he didn't know he had a brother, but he could certainly use the money. An odd couple, the rich man and the poor man. They are bound to each other, for not only is poor Andreas happy about his unexpected rescue from need, his rich brother insists that he counts himself fortunate to be able to give some of his money to the poor man. And something else binds these brothers together: it is not only Andreas who camps out under bridges without house or home; the seemingly rich gentleman is another traveling man who lives under bridges. So for a time miracle succeeds miracle in this last book of Joseph Roth's. Until the miracles run out.

. . .

When Joseph Roth gets the news in Paris in May 1939 that Ernst Toller has committed suicide in his hotel room in New York, he breaks down. Friderike Zweig, who's with him, has him taken to a hospital, where he dies a few days later. Stefan Zweig hears of this in London as he is writing to Romain Rolland. "We will not grow old, we exiles," he writes, shattered. "I loved him like a brother."

· · ·

OSTEND NO LONGER EXISTS. There's another city today, a new one with the same name. The German troops marched into Ostend on May 29, 1940. They met with no resistance. In 1944 the Allied forces flew numerous missions that almost reduced the city to nothing. Today a pathetic fragment of the station façade can still be seen, but the promenade along the beach is strewn with white, faceless buildings. The boulevard is as broad as it once was, paved in red bricks. Concrete benches stand around everywhere, and no one sits on them. It's November 2012, the sky is gray, the place is empty of people. The Hôtel de la Couronne has disappeared, in its place a dark apartment house called the Riviera. Next to it is an empty building site—you can see the wallpaper in the neighboring house, with gray flowers on the wall. Sailboats in the harbor. Nobody's sailing them. Then, by the sea, where the Maison Floréal once stood, there's a functional building from the 1960s; on the fourth floor, at the level of the former loggia, there's a garishly colored sign, "Te Huur," to rent.

In the Langestraat, where Almondo served pasta to his two famous guests, there's now a dark pub, called Manuscript; the friendly waiter is already drunk in the afternoon and skims the foam off the beer glasses in the Belgian fashion with a wooden stick. The sound system is playing "Crazy Mama" by J. J. Cale, Elvis Presley's "That's All Right," Louis Prima's "Sing, Sing, Sing," and "Mystery Train" by Paul Butterfield. Four men are sitting silently at the bar. They make you think they live here. The sea is gray and flat, great green breakwaters reach down into the waves, the beach is wide and empty. No bathing huts, but a few early Christmas trees in the wind. In one of the cul-de-sacs leading down off the promenade, an old, narrow house. In the window, masks, starfish on invisible threads, and shells. Inside a counter made of dark wood, more masks, old photos on the walls. A red-carpeted staircase leads up past a small kitchen with red enameled pots on the stove to the room, and the piano is there, and the painting with the deathly procession that covers one entire wall. A vase with dusty grasses, another with a skull and a lady's hat on top; a picture in a photo album shows the distraught old painter in the ruins of his hometown. James Ensor's house. It is one of the few houses from the old times still standing today.

And the people?

Egon Erwin Kisch went to New York, then Mexico, then back to New York after the war, then returned to his home city of Prague, where he died in 1948 in the aftermath of two heart attacks. Six horses pulled the bier with his coffin through the streets of the city while traffic came to a halt. At the end of the funeral service, the "Internationale" was sung. Arthur Koestler succeeded in penetrating Franco's headquarters, was arrested, spent three months on death row, escaped, went to London, repudiated Communism, wrote the epochal *Darkness at Noon*, and on March 3, 1983, committed joint suicide with his wife, Cynthia. On November 27, 1916, Émile Verhaeren slipped while boarding a train in Rouen, where he had delivered an anti-German lecture about the war, and was run over by the departing carriage. The family declined an offer to have him interred in the Pantheon and buried him in the military cemetery at Adinkerke instead. He was soon dug up again out of fear of the advancing German troops and transferred to the security of Wulveringen; from there his body was moved again in 1927 to his final resting place in his original home of Sint-Amands. Friedl Roth, after her parents emigrated to Palestine, was moved from the Steinhof psychiatric hospital to the regional care facility of Mauer-Oehling. In 1940 she was moved to a clinic in Linz, where she was murdered in June of that year pursuant to the National Socialist euthanasia program. Irmgard Keun went into hiding in Holland when the German troops invaded in May 1940. She had lost forty pounds, drank constantly, and was sometimes to be seen in the street and sometimes in a pub. She wanted to go back to Cologne. Her brother wrote to a friend: "What's going to happen to her, as a purely practical matter, is something more or less unimaginable to me. What she's written is all too clearly hostile, and will hardly be forgiven. I'm appalled that fate takes a life made up of such a mixture of foolishness and honorable endeavors and makes it a capital matter." She succeeded in going back. A Nazi literary publication triumphantly announced her suicide, but she lived, secretly, in Germany, for years even after the war, forgotten by her readers. At the end of the 1970s, her work was rediscovered thanks to the journalist Jürgen Serke. The last three years of her life, to her astonishment, were a kind of small literary triumphant procession. She died on May 5, 1982. Christiane Grautoff lived a life that was like a novel. She had many husbands, many lovers, and many friends. She died on August 27, 1974, in her apartment in Mexico City, so peacefully that her granddaughter Christiane, who was bouncing around on the bed, didn't even notice. She had written an account of her life shortly before. A piece of paper was found on her deathbed, with the words, in English: "The one and only reason I wrote my autobiography with all my blood and sweat is—" Willi Muenzenberg left the Communist Party in March 1939. In May 1940 he let himself be interned in the Stade de Colombe, a vacation camp that had hosted soccer games for the World Cup not two years previously. He hoped this would lead to his transfer to the southern part of France. His plan went into motion; he set off for Chambaran, near Lyon, in a column that also included the journalist Leopold Schwarzschild, the publisher Kurt Wolff, and many others. On June 12 he separated from the column. On October 17 his body was found with a noose around the neck in a forest near Charmes. He had been dead since June 21 or 22. Otto Katz spent his life in service of the Party, was active in building up the Communist Party in Czechoslovakia, and in 1952, along with numerous comrades of mostly Jewish origin, was put on trial and sentenced to death. His ashes were reputedly mixed with winter road grit and scattered on the streets of Prague. Despite international protests, Etkar André was beheaded on November 4, 1936. The five thousand inmates of Fuhlsbuettel Prison thereupon went on strike; the burial had to take place in strictest secrecy by orders of the Gestapo. Stefan and Lotte Zweig moved into the little house in Petrópolis. This was where Stefan Zweig wrote *Chess Story* and finished *The World of Yesterday*. On February 22, 1942, he writes a farewell letter to the world, heading it *Declaração*. "I greet all my friends! May they all see the glow of dawn after the long night! I, all too impatient, am going on ahead." He doesn't mention Lotte. No farewell letter from her was found. The longest survivor was Hermann Kesten. He became an

American citizen, lived in New York, later in Rome, and finally in Basel. The young German writers had no interest in him. The head of Group 47,* Hans Werner Richter, who didn't want to have any émigrés in the group, did actually invite Kesten and the critic Hans Sahl one time. A mistake, as the former Wehrmacht soldier Richter wrote in his diary: "Neither of them tolerated any criticism, both were full of sensitive, idiotic vanity, both were expecting [we'd have] guilt complexes." Kesten himself, in an assessment he made of German literature in 1965, complained of "a certain intolerance (among the new German writers) for the former exiled authors, whom they no longer consider to be part of German literature or consign to a kind of ghetto. Certainly a little group of the formerly exiled authors is somewhat sensitive, that is, those who are still alive." Kesten died in 1996. He was ninety-six years old. James Ensor died in November 19, 1949, in his hometown, at the age of eighty-nine. He is buried in the graveyard on the dunes in Ostend. From up there you have a beautiful view of the sea.

*The group of young writers after the war who came to symbolize the new German literature.

Stefan Zweig (left) and Joseph Roth in Ostend, Belgium, January 1936
(Photo by Imagno/Getty Images)

A NOTE ON THE TYPE

This book was set in a typeface called Berling, designed by the Swedish typographer Karl-Erik Forsberg (1914–1995). Berling is named after the foundry that produced it, Berlingska Stilgjuteriet of Lund, and was first used to produce *The Rembrandt Bible* in 1954.

Composed by North Market Street Graphics, Lancaster, Pennsylvania

Printed and bound by RR Donnelley, Harrisonburg, Virginia

Designed by M. Kristen Bearse